God in You!
"Ps, 18:19"

THE LORD'S PRAYER-
REVISITED

SEVEN WAYS TO DELIVERANCE

To: Megan
With Love
Be Blessed!
"Madie"

THE LORD'S PRAYER-REVISITED

SEVEN WAYS TO DELIVERANCE

Carolyn Chambers

The Lord's Prayer - Revisited
Seven Ways to Deliverance

Printed in the United States of America
Library of Congress Cataloging-In-Publication Data
Chambers, Carolyn

The Lord's Prayer – Revisited / Carolyn Chambers
p. cm Library of Congress Control Number: 1-3530722361

ISBN: Softcover   978-0-9967582-1-5

1. Ministry
2. Religion
3. Self Help

Editing and book design by Keith H. Chambers
Cover Design by C W Technology Consulting

www.anointedlifepublishing.com

Dedication

This book is dedicated to my parents and in-laws, for giving me a
lifetime of fond memories.

Where there is no vision,
the people perish:
but he that keepeth the law,
happy is he.

(Proverbs 29:18, King James Version)

Contents

The LORD shall cause thine enemies that rise up against thee to be smitten before thy face: they shall come out against thee one way, and flee before thee seven ways.

(Deuteronomy 28:7)

Preface

The Lord's Prayer: God's Marital Duty
A Stealth Operation

It is the upsets in life that can be devastating and at times even catastrophic, concerning our faith. You prayed for the job of your choice, but you were turned down; you prayed that a relationship would survive, but it failed; you prayed that a loved one would recover, but they passed. In other words, you expected God's perfect will, but you got His acceptable will. Each setback weakens your confidence and strengthens the perception that you never know what to expect from your prayers.

Years ago, I was in a similar predicament. I found myself falling prey to disappointment after disappointment—I just did not see the manifestation of my faith. Fortunately, the Holy Spirit impressed upon me the need to pray the Lord's Prayer; with special emphasis on the part that says, "...*deliver us from evil.*" The turnaround was immediate. The Lord's Prayer prepared me for the upset! It kept me from yielding to the devices of the wicked.

In praying the Lord's Prayer, I found myself doing the right thing at the right time; particularly, 'proving all things.' This alone, weakened the element of surprise and disarmed the weapon of disappointment. Now, it is a safeguard for me. I have found it to be especially helpful in heeding Jesus' directive, *"Take heed therefore that the light which is in thee be not darkness"* (Luke 11:35). This scripture refers to times when we earnestly think that we are right, but we are missing the mark.

There are three important tenants regarding the Lord's Prayer:

1. The Lord's Prayer is His marital duty: God is *betrothed* to us in righteousness, in judgment, in lovingkindness, and in mercies. (Hosea 2:19)

2. The Lord's Prayer is a type of stealth (secret) operation: *"You will not see wind, neither rain,* yet *the valleys shall be filled with water..."* (2Kings 3:17).

3. The Lord's Prayer is a covering: It causes all the tests, trials, and temptations we face, to hit Him first! (Deuteronomy 9:3)

In Jeremiah 9:23-24, the Lord explains the delight He feels in being there for His people, saying, *"...I am the LORD which exercise lovingkindness, judgment, and righteousness, in the earth: for in these things I delight, saith the LORD."* Because our Maker is our Husband, performing His marital duty *is* His delight! This call of duty allows God to do what He does best: bless His children.

Deuteronomy 28:1-14, shows the blessings that shall come on us and overtake us as a result of Christ redeeming us from the curse of the law. Verse 7 is my favorite: *"The LORD shall cause thine enemies that rise up against thee to be smitten before thy face: they shall come out against thee one way, and flee before thee seven ways."*

It was after confessing this promise faithfully, for many years, that the Holy Spirit said to me, "I have seven ways to deliver you." This revelation alone, blessed me. But it was not until recently that He connected the seven ways of deliverance to each *petition* (verse) of the Lord's Prayer; thus bringing me into some of its inner workings.

More importantly, I also discovered that when our prayers are ineffective, we can usually find, in one of those seven ways, where we went astray. *This book is a result of that Revelation.*

Acknowledgements

Special thanks to the multitude of counselors. Through you, I found encouragement in penning the words of this book.

Special thanks to my husband, Keith. You turn the ordinary into the extraordinary...you have no competition; you are one of a kind.

Special Thanks also to the Comforter; it is such a delight to have you in my life.

Can two walk together,
except they be agreed?

(Amos 3:3)

Introduction

The Analysis of Un-answered Prayer

The Need:	To hear from God
The Supply:	God sends the answer
The Test:	Heart rejects the answer
The Cause:	Identity issues
The Effect:	Can't function in God's likeness
The Attack:	Rains on the just and unjust
The Problem:	Not prepared for the storm
The Result:	Go around the mountain another year

As the Shepherd of our souls, God knows what things we have need of. As Father, He has also supplied the need; however, because of the condition of our hearts, the supply is often met with opposition. Because of unbelief, three out of four of us will reject the wisdom sown in our hearts. This occurs primarily because our identity (who we are in Christ) has not been established; making us ill-prepared to function in His likeness; to think like Him. Consequently, we are not equipped to handle the storms of life. Then, finding ourselves going around the same mountain again and again, we sit back and question God. But through praying the Lord's Prayer, our Maker can get in and turn things around.

The Lord's Prayer-Revisited focuses on *seven* ways God uses to bring about a turnaround in our prayer lives.

First, it brings us back to God's original manner of prayer; it teaches us to prepare our hearts to receive His Word and to keep it. Next, it helps to guard us from the sin of presumption that leads to unbelief and ultimate disappointment.

1

The Lord's Prayer also teaches us that prayer is a <u>test</u> that exposes the condition of our hearts. God is endeavoring to prove Himself faithful to those whose hearts are perfect toward Him. But often, His Word finds no rest in many of our hearts.

To adjust our hearts, The Lord's Prayer-Revisited addresses the following:

- *Seven Hindrances* of each prayer petition—the areas where we fall short of the glory of God; *missing the mark.*

- Seven *Strategies*—ways to become spiritually empowered to *escape* the hindrance.

- Seven Processes of Recovery—these enable us to *think* on God's level; function in *His likeness.*

- *Seven biblical Types of Prayer*—to cover all bases; as we pray each prayer, we give God access to work supernaturally in all areas of our lives.

- Seven Redemptive Names of God—where the benefits and promises of God are confirmed in each name. There has not failed one word of all God's good promises.

Finally, The Lord's Prayer-Revisited will help you to think thoughts that allow virtue to flow and address the enemy of our faith; thereby giving God's Word free course to manifest on our behalf.

Answered prayer is our inheritance. It is the children's bread. Being faithful, God has done His part, and His Word, which cannot return void, *hovers*—awaiting our response. It's our *turn.*

2

The Answer vs. the Solution

Understanding is the key to whether we have solutions in life or just answers. When the evil spirit troubled King Saul (Israel's first king), music played by David drove the evil spirit away. That was the answer, but it was not the solution, as David had to serve King Saul in this manner often.

Being unwise, King Saul never understood the will of God. He admitted that he obeyed the people instead of God. Because of his failure to do God's commandment, God *removed him and found David, a man after His own heart, which shall fulfil all of His will.* (Acts 13:22)

Lack of understanding was also the key that caused the wayside ground to be unfruitful. (Matthew 13) The people allowed the fowls of the air to steal the Word that had been sown in their hearts. On the other hand, Job asked to be given understanding to see where he had erred. (Job 6:24)

In understanding, we are exhorted to be men; not children. In Nehemiah 8:7, the leaders caused the people to understand the law, and the people *stood* in their place. Also, when Gideon and his men *stood, every man in his place of authority, the enemy ran, and cried, and fled.* [1] And, prior to taking Jericho, the priest's feet stood firm and caused the waters to be cut off, and the people passed over—*right against Jericho.* When we stand, holding our peace, the enemy stands down.

In the same manner, when we understand the <u>inner workings</u> of the Lord's Prayer, it will cause *us* to stand in our place of authority, as well. We stand on the promises of God, stand on the Word of God, and stand as we work our covenant.

Whereas praying the Lord's Prayer is the answer; understanding the Lord's Prayer is the solution.

The Intrigue of the Lord's Prayer

The intrigue of the Lord's Prayer lies in Matthew 6:8, where Jesus says, *"... for your Father knoweth what things you have need of, before you ask Him."* That begs the question: Why then do we need to ask Him? I pondered this for some time, and frustrated, I finally did what the Bible said to do, which is, ask your husband. God promptly gave my husband, Keith, a one word revelation: *agreement.*

At the heart of the Lord's Prayer is agreement between God and man and heaven and earth. It is a vertical agreement between God and man where <u>discernment</u> (perception of the obscure) is required. God is looking for the spirit of man to be involved in the decisions we make.

God, the Father, being a good Father, has seen the need. But for heaven to intervene on our behalf, agreement is required. So, the *secret* to answered prayer is the *test of agreement.* And, when we say what God says (echo His heart), we pass the test!

Adam passed God's test:

Before the fall, Adam worked the Process of Discerning Agreement to perfection. Knowing what we have need of before we ask, God identified an area of need for Adam:

- God said*: "It is not good that the man should be alone;"*
- God also identified the supply: *"I will make him an help meet for him."*
- The test began: God brought all the animals before Adam, *"...to see what he would call them: And whatsoever Adam called every living creature that was the name thereof. And Adam gave names to all cattle, and to the fowl of the air, and to every beast of the field"* (Genesis 2:18-20).

4

It was after all the work of naming all the cattle, the fowl of the air (an enemy of the Word of God), and every beast of the field that the Bible said:

- *"...But for Adam there was not found an help meet for him."*

Using discernment, Adam found nothing else made in God's image.

- Adam passed God's test! He echoed God's heart.

Now, there was agreement between heaven and earth! And, God could intervene on Adam's behalf. So, God went to work on answering his prayer, allowing God's will to be done in earth as it is in heaven. God and Adam were seeing eye-to-eye; because Adam walked in his identity, that made the *test of agreement* easy.

Adam's fall from agreement:

Unfortunately, Adam does not continue to echo God's heart. He commits an error of omission. After the 'excitement' of receiving his help meet, Adam failed to name her. He called her Woman. [2] That is <u>what</u> she was but not <u>who</u> she was; 'woman' does not connect her to her spiritual identity. Without an identity, she could not walk in her authority—she literally could not help herself. Eve was subject to deception, because her spirit was not involved in the decision. Instead, she leaned to her own understanding and soon fell prey to the influence of the enemy—a victim of doubt, unbelief, and fear.

To Adam's credit, after the curse was pronounced, he realized his error, repented, and called her name, Eve (the mother of 'all living'). (Genesis 3:20) She then had her spiritual identity and that gave her purpose, ability, and authority.

Eve's plight was not unique to her. As a young Christian, I too, lacked spiritual identity, and I could not help myself. For days, I had tormenting nightmares of an airplane crashing into the back yard of my house. When I shared this dream with a couple of born again saints, they told me who I was in Christ; even telling me that God had *not* given me a spirit of fear. I went home that night and before retiring, I spoke to the attack saying, "In Jesus' name, I will not have another nightmare." And the nightmares stopped!

Because all of our enemies are not natural, our identity is needed to help us operate in our spiritual authority. Our spiritual identity enables us to function in His likeness and walk in our dominion. Without it, we will operate in *unbelief.*

Unbelief Attacks

Unbelief is the sin from which all other sins flow—it is believing something God did not say. And, it separates us from our anointing.

Unbelief negates our spiritual identity:

In the New Testament, 3 Mary Magdalene found herself in a similar identity issue as Eve. Being the first to go to Jesus' tomb, Mary Magdalene found it empty. Walking by sight, she assumed someone had stolen Him, but receiving this thought placed her in the flesh; *alienated* from her spirit and subject to unbelief. And, Jesus, not knowing her by the flesh, addressed her, calling her *woman.* She, being in the flesh, also didn't recognize Him. And, because she was in unbelief, she assumed that He was the gardener.

Jesus then received a word of knowledge of her true identity, and He then called her by name: "Mary." The Bible said she *turned* herself, and saw Him no longer as a gardener but as Jesus; she then called Him, Rabboni—which is to say, Master.

Our name connects us our spiritual identity; Jesus said he calls His own sheep by name, "...*and leadeth them out*" (John 10:3). Jesus, addressing Mary by name, brought her out from under the influence of the flesh and back to the influence of her spirit.

Unbelief and the process of turning:

The thoughts we receive will either place us in our spirit or in our flesh. We are either *turning* to obey thoughts from our spirit, or we are *turning* to obey thoughts from our flesh. And, when we turn, we begin to think and ultimately speak out thoughts of doubt and unbelief.

It is interesting to note that according to Mark 16:7, Mary had been told that Jesus would die and be raised from the dead on the third day, but she did not keep (guard) the Word that had been sown in her heart. Failing to keep this Word caused her to *turn* and yield to unbelief, and it is unbelief that distorts our perception of life and of each other. According to John 20:8, the disciple, John saw the same empty tomb, but he believed. He did not turn.

Unbelief vs. whose we are:

Unbelief also affects our sense of belonging as it perverts our identity relative to whose we are. Luke 19 tells the story of Zacchaeus, who was rich and seemed to have had it all together. Yet, he too suffered from an identity issue. Jesus had to bring salvation to his house, stating that he too was a son of Abraham.

Unbelief attacks the supply:

Because God sees the need, He sows the seed. But unfortunately, because of the condition of our souls, His word finds no place in many of our hearts; it has to compete with our own philosophy and vain deceit.

A couple sensed the need to relocate but felt that they had not heard from God. Nevertheless, God had seen the need and had spoken to each of their hearts. But the answer was not pleasant, so it was rejected. God's counsel came up against their philosophy (system of thought) and was therefore not received as a viable option. Eventually, they turned from their unbelief and were blessed.

Unbelief attacks the ground:

In the parable of the sower, Jesus explained the impact of unbelief on our hearts (the ground) as he addressed the concept of the sower sows the seed; 4 the seed is the Word of God.

- When the seed was sown by the way side, they heard the Word, but because they did not understand it, the fowls of the air devoured the Word that had been sown in their hearts.
- When the seed was sown on rocky ground, they too heard the Word, but became offended, so the seed was unfruitful.
- The sower also sowed it on thorny ground. They admitted to hearing it, but the Word was choked with cares and the lust of other things and brought no fruit to fruition.
- But when the same seed was sown on good ground, those with an honest and good heart heard the Word and kept (guarded) it, and brought forth fruit.

The good ground, you could say, saw the Word as a treasure, 5 so they prepared their hearts to keep it; however, not without a fight. First they had to *sell* their: unbelief, fears, cares, doubt, and lust. They leaned not to their own understanding, and they *bought* the truth. Because they refused to give up the seed, they were then prepared to handle the storms of life (that come to both the just and the unjust).

Those whose houses fell during the storm were *called* hearers only and *named* foolish. Being hearers only, they were self-deceived; not able to bear the storm. They let their houses fall into confusion and were never able to bring in a harvest. But those who kept the seed (Word) and beared the storm were *called* hearers and doers and *named* wise. What *we* are called and named plays an important role in our ability to weather the storms of life.

Unbelief and our prayer life:

An evil heart of unbelief will impact our prayer life, also. For, praying as children, rather than exercising sonship, affects our ability to discern good and bad; it hinders the test of agreement, and prevents God from intervening on our behalf. When we pray, leaning to our own understanding, or trusting in our own hearts, and not in the Word of God, it is unbelief; our prayers become ineffectual.

While praying for finances, I went to the man of God and asked him to touch and agree with me for my finances to flow. He spoke a word of wisdom—informing me that the Holy Spirit said, *"You don't need money, you need resources."* I had been leaning to my own understanding. When I got the unbelief out, I began to prosper.

A Perfect Storm

You can see how important the role of identity plays in a person's life. But for Eve, the lack of identity was only half of the battle. Eve entered into what I call a perfect storm.

In Genesis 2:15, God gave the man the responsibility of guarding his heart. It was his only duty: to dress the garden (heart) and keep (guard) it. According to the New Testament, the dressing involved insuring a production of *fruit*.[6] This fruit is the 'fruit of the Spirit' and is identified as: love, joy, peace, patience, kindness, goodness, faith, meekness, and temperance. If none is found, the heart is vulnerable; subject to corruption. The fruit provides protection against attacks by our carnal nature. Galatians 5:22-23, says: The fruit guards against the law (flesh). With the fruit of the Spirit you are *dressed* for battle.

But Adam failed to guard his heart; the Bible said the *man* and the *woman* were both naked—they were fruitless. Consequently, the woman (Eve) could not partake of *his divine nature* and escape the corruption [7] that she found herself confronted with. It was a perfect storm: She could not help herself; yet she found no help in *man*. In a perfect world, even being without an identity, she could have partaken of his peace—a fruit of the Spirit, or his temperance—also a fruit of the Spirit. Any fruit would have strengthened her against the contaminating influences of the carnal nature. But that was not the case.

Others have benefited greatly from partaking of the fruit. Consider the prodigal son. [8] The father's love (a fruit of the Spirit) allowed the son to come to himself and return home. The Bible says that the father had compassion on him while he was still yet a long way off.

The *lack* of fruit also represents a challenge for *us* in our everyday lives. How many times do we find our loved ones in a prodigal situation, with no way to return home, because they find no fruit? One of my favorite stories is about a nephew, who found himself in a dishonorable situation with his mother. Yet he not only prospered, he excelled. Puzzled, I asked God why this was so when clearly the Bible says it should *not* be well with him. The Holy Spirit said that it was because his mother never held it against him. She kept her love so that he could find his way back. Recently, this nephew called to say that he had given his mother a warm, heart-felt apology.

The voice and the choice:

The attack against Eve was two-fold: She lacked an identity and she could not partake of Adam's fruit of the Spirit. We know that Eve was first drawn away of her own lust [9] (desire) and enticed. She had already fallen away, [10] because of unbelief, and finding no fruit, she had no way of escape. So, the curse came. And in addressing the cause of the curse, God did the following:

- First He dealt with the voice: *"Who told you that you were naked?"* God observed that no discernment was used. So, the blind was leading the blind.

- Then He questioned their choice: *"Have you eaten of the tree wherein I commanded you not to?"*[11] They ate the fruit of unbelief. The spirit was not involved in this decision.

God then explained that there would now be enmity between the enemy and the woman; between his seed and her Seed—it will be a battle to enter into His rest. We will have to fight thoughts of doubt, fear, and unbelief, which oppose the <u>Process of Agreement</u>. We would also have to *call* and *name* the many inner and outer voices coming against us. But ultimately, the Seed (the Word of God), shall bruise the enemy's head as we render judgment on each thought, taking it captive.

Jesus followed the same process in John 8:44. Discerning good and bad, He exercised judgment against the voices that were coming against Him: He *called* him the *Devil* and *named* him the father of lies. By doing so, Jesus met the criteria of *discernment agreement* with the Father. He did not allow Himself to become *seduced* by the 'many voices.' Jesus knew that in dealing with the voice, He would not make the wrong choice.

Introduction

1. Judges 7:21
2. Genesis 2:23
3. John 20
4. Luke 8:5-15; Matthew 13:18-23; Mark 4:3-20
5. Matthew 13:44
6. Luke 13:6-9
7. 2 Peter 1:4
8. Luke 15
9. James 1:14
10. 2 Thessalonians 2:3
11. Genesis 3:11

Our Father
which art in heaven,
Hallowed be thy name.

Chapter 1

Deliverance through Sonship

*O*ur Father which art in heaven, Hallowed be thy name, is the petition that evokes the Prayer of Agreement, examining our walk of agreement. Through this prayer, we call on Jehovah Shammah - the God who is always there. The strategy for this petition addresses our identity relative to our relationship to the Father—specifically, sonship (a call to maturity). God is looking for a Father-son connection: co-laborers. Operating the Process of Discernment Agreement, we call Him, Father...

A young man was complaining that God never answered his prayers. I naturally assumed that he was coming to the Father in the name of Jesus, but that was not the case. He was addressing the Father as God. He was out of agreement. Understanding where he had erred, I suggested that he call Him Father. He agreed to try it. At our next meeting, he was all smiles. Addressing God as 'Father' had made the difference! He talked of how God had manifested Himself to him for the first time in his life.

The Father-son connection had been made; and agreement was in place. Now God could begin to intervene on his behalf. And of course, this constituted the beginning of the end for the enemy. In teaching His disciples to pray, Jesus began with acknowledging God as Father.

The Hindrance to the Petition
(King is a Child) [1]

We miss it on this level when we either fail to identify with God as our Father, or being a child, we lack growth and maturity. Although He is still Father, operating as a child, you may not be able to partake of your full inheritance. When the king is a child, he differs nothing from a slave (servant) though he is Lord of all. [2] He cannot represent the Father's heart; he is in bondage to a slave mentality and shares its identity. Also, when the king is a child, the prince of the power of the air will find childish things that have not yet been put away, such as: anger, malice, wrath, bitterness, and fear—these, of course, hinder us from exercising kingdom dominion:

- As children, walking by sight, we may see the giants in the land. But as sons, we confess that we are well able to take the land, because God is with us.
- As children, following our feelings, we may feel that we are the least in our father's house. But as sons, we see ourselves as mighty men and women of valor.
- As children, being fearful, we may find ourselves going around the same mountain for forty years. But as sons, we say, "Give me this mountain!"

God is endeavoring to *be* a Father to us. The call to sonship is a call for us to change our perception of ourselves and be no more children tossed to and fro by every wind of doctrine. [3] When we touch *not* the unclean thing (unbelief), the Father will receive us. He will *be* a Father unto us, and we shall be His sons and daughters. [4] Sons do not beg; they come boldly to the throne of grace. [5]

Hebrews 5:2 speaks of the compassion God has on the ignorant and on those that are out of the way (wayward). So, even when we miss it, we can still come boldly to the throne of grace to obtain mercy and find grace to help in times of need.

The Strategy to Escape the Hindrance
(Sonship)

Sonship is a call to be who we are. As born again children of God, we have received the power to become sons of God; [6] however, sonship is a growth process. Jesus grew in stature, wisdom, and favor with God and man.[7] And when the growth process is embraced, *we grow in grace, and in the knowledge of our Lord and Savior, Jesus Christ.*[8] According to Romans 8:14, the process is easy: *"For as many as are led by the Spirit of God, they are the sons of God."*

The Holy Spirit is our Helper. Consequently, He wants to be personally involved in all areas of our lives; even the minor details of life. He is there to satisfy our souls in drought. [9] It is the Holy Spirit who gives us the unction to know all things, [10] and to receive our inheritance, He must lead us in the way that we should go.

Sonship was conferred on Jesus after the Holy Spirit descended on Him.[11] Simply put, sons are those who allow themselves to be *led* by the still waters. Sons are then prepared to execute judgment in the morning against the enemy, and they deliver the spoiled out of the hands of the oppressor. [12] They execute judgment of truth and peace. God promises to give the Holy Spirit to them that ask Him.[13]

No condemnation:

When we pray: *Our Father which art in heaven, Hallowed be thy name,* we also activate the unconditional covenant ratified by our Lord and Saviour, Jesus Christ, on the cross. Jesus fulfilled the promise of the terms of the covenant by living a perfect life. He also satisfied the terms of the curse by His sacrificial death on the cross, for our sins. The fact is, we have been blessed and it can't be reversed. [14] We are now made the righteousness of God by faith in Jesus Christ. It is for all who believe.[15] We are qualified by believing. Being made righteous, there is therefore now no condemnation to them that are in Christ Jesus; the law of the spirit of life in Christ Jesus has made us free from the law of sin and death, [16]

Being made free from condemnation, we are required keep feelings of regret, guilt, and sorrow out of our hearts. Those are some of the contaminating influences that inhibit us from coming boldly to the throne of grace.

Finally, forgoing condemnation, we never give up on ourselves or others; God has made provision for our salvation, as well as for our mistakes. Remember, He turns our mistakes into miracles.

Hallowed be thy name—Seven redemptive names:

It is the Seven Redemptive Names of God that allow us to hallow His Name—where the benefits and promises of God are confirmed. According to one Bible teacher, the Name of Jesus embodies all the essence, characteristics, and power evoked in each of Jehovah's Redemptive Names.

The Bible says: *"And they that know thy name will put their trust in thee..."* (Psalms 9:10). As we *hallow* His Name, we make a demand on the promises and attributes His Name denotes, and because we belong to Him, we are *kept* in His Name. His Name is a strong tower, where the righteous run into it and are safe. (Proverbs 18:10)

As sons, we bask in exalting His Name during our time of prayer. Being thankful blesses His Name. (Psalms 100:4) Singing unto the Lord blesses His Name. (Psalms 96:2) Moreover, we hallow His Name as we remember all of His benefits: He forgives, heals, redeems, crowns, satisfies, and executes righteousness and judgment for all who are oppressed. (Psalms 103) Finally, when we extol Him, we bless His Name; we lift His Name on high. (Psalms 145:1)

The Process of Discernment Agreement
Calling and Naming

(Guarding Your Identity)

This process focuses on the ability to *discern* between good and bad. When we walk as sons, this process <u>guards</u> our identity.

The Discerning Alert
1 Kings 3:9

- Wisdom (what): *"Give therefore thy servant an understanding heart*
- Understanding (why): *to judge thy people*
- Knowledge (how): *that I may discern between good and bad."*

After receiving this gift, King Solomon used it to discern deceit. By doing so, he walked in agreement with God. When the two women, both of whom claimed to be the mother of the same child, came before King Solomon seeking justice, 17 he tested their love. When he discerned love, he knew which one had the heart of the Father and which one was an imposter. Discerning both good and bad is the essence of this process and is required to walk in agreement with God, as a son.

In the book of 2 Samuel 3:12-34, the captain of Saul's army, Abner, was in the process of making a league with King David, in hopes of unifying the kingdom. But David's general, Joab, had a secret quarrel with Abner. After a meeting between King David and Abner, Joab pretended to befriend Abner. The Bible said he took him aside to speak with him quietly; instead he killed him (to avenge his brother).

As King David lamented over Abner, he said Abner died as a fool dies. A fool simply assumes. Abner failed to discern between good and bad. And because he was not sober and vigilant, he could not render judgment. He did not discern the heart of God, nor his conscience, relative to Joab's motive. And so the process of agreement was not met.

Our Father Which Art In Heaven, Hallowed Be Thy Name

Key elements of this petition:

The Hindrance to this petition lies in a failure to see ourselves the way God sees us. Our prayers must be based on sonship—sons of God—joint heirs with Christ.

The Strategy requires that the spirit becomes an integral part of our decision-making process. As the candle of the Lord, God uses our spirit to enlighten us. (Proverbs 20:27) It helps us to bear fruit and glorify God. It keeps us from walking as mere men.

Through the Process of Discernment, we view things from a proper perspective—God's point of view. Calling and naming the many voices confronting us, may even involve *calling those things that be not as though they were*, to walk in our identity. (Romans 4:17) I'm thinking of Abraham. Fighting the contradiction of being childless, he called himself the father of many nations. God honored his confession of faith.

This petition also requires an identity check-up, including routing the enemy of your faith: doubt, unbelief, and fear.

Our Father which art in heaven, Hallowed be thy name, identifies us as sons with full rights and privileges of sonship; giving the Prayer of Agreement the power to call it done; being empowered by Jehovah Shammah - the God who is always there.

The Prayer of Agreement

This prayer connects us to the power of united prayer, where one can chase a thousand, but two can put ten thousand to flight. The enemy does not fight fair. But Psalms 55:18 says: *"... he has delivered my soul in peace from the battle that was against me: for there were many with me."* This prayer evens the odds. It brings in the concept of a multitude of counselors and stands against unilateral decision making; placing the rule of law over arbitrary decisions. It also presupposes that a vertical agreement is already in place—mainly, that our actions are in agreement with God and His Word.

Matthew 18:19-20

- Wisdom (what): *"Again I say unto you, That if two of you shall agree on earth as touching anything that they shall ask,*
- Understanding (why): *it shall be done for them of my Father which is in heaven.*
- Knowledge (how): *For where two or three are gathered together in my name, there am I in the midst of them."*

Walking in agreement on earth:

After suffering from 3rd degree burns, my brother was left with one very large open wound on his leg, about the size of a lemon. He went home from the hospital; then was scheduled for *monthly* follow-up visits at the burn center. We understood that when significant progress was made, we would only have to come *quarterly*. I monitored and changed his dressing on a regular basis. Finally, after a time, the wound began to heal.

On a subsequent visit to the burn center, after the wound had reduced considerably in size, a new physician's assistant instructed me to discontinue the regular wound dressing and instead only keep the wound lubricated. But I had faith in the dressing that we had been using.

So, I was not in agreement with her solution, and I decided to continue with the regular treatment. The next day I noticed that rather than getting better, the wound had got worse. At the same time, the Holy Spirit spoke to me and said, "All healing comes from God." Then I remembered the scriptures: *"Can two walk together unless they be agreed?"* [18] And, *"...a house divided cannot stand."* [19] I realized that I was out of agreement and quickly made the decision to follow the PA's instructions.

The next day, I noticed an immediate change. I knew the wound was healed—yet in the natural, soft tissue was still visible. So, continuing my faith walk, I spoke to the situation saying, "When we return to the burn clinic, they will agree that the wound is healed and that we will be upgraded to three-month follow-up visits."

When we arrived, the PA examined the wound, as I shared with her my faith of not having to return for three months. She left the room, then came back and said, "I agree. You will not have to return for three months." Three days later, I noticed that the wound site had blended in with his normal body tissue. Until she agreed, the wound was under siege, awaiting confirmation. We then met the criteria of two on earth walking in agreement, and God called it done.

Walking in agreement with God:

Years ago, following my devotion, God gave me a plan that would enable me to make my sales quota. Although I was a young Christian, I heard His voice and understood fully. As I started my walk with God, executing His plan, a thought came to me of a *better* way. All of a sudden, God's way seemed foolish and impractical. But when I began exercising the *better* way, I noticed that I wasn't getting any results. So I quickly changed plans; did it God's way, and I was able to make the necessary sales. My provision was tied to walking in agreement with God.

God knows where the fish are, also. Jesus told Peter to let down his nets on the other side. This logic seemed foolish to Peter who had been fishing all night and caught nothing. But Peter said, *"Nevertheless at thy Word I will let down the net."* [20] He caught a net-breaking boatload of fish when he agreed with Jesus.

The Prayer of Agreement activates the commanded blessing and <u>connects</u> us to the <u>faith of others</u>. When we are young, God puts us under a guardian: parent, a teacher, a caretaker, a voice, or even a mentor. As we learn to follow their voice of wisdom, we *progress* to hearing God's voice and walking in agreement with Him. This, in turn, causes others to walk in favor with us.

Walking in agreement saves lives:

In the book of Esther, Esther's fame can be traced back to her walking in agreement with those who had been placed over her. The Bible says, *"... she required nothing but what Hegai the king's chamberlain, the keeper of the woman, appointed."* [21] The Bible says she obtained kindness of him

Regarding her cousin Mortdecai, the Bible says: *"...for Esther did the commandment of Mordecai, like as when she was brought up with him."*[22] We all know how it ends. She married the king and later asked him to save her people. The king followed her lead and granted her petition.

Esther's predecessor, Queen Vashti, refused to walk in agreement with the king, and she was deposed from her position of power. [23]

Walking in agreement releases power and promotion:

In the book of Ruth, Naomi gave Ruth a list of instructions, to which Ruth replied, *"<u>All</u> that thou sayest unto me I will do."* And this was not just lip service. Ruth performed each task, because she did not have her own agenda.

21

What is interesting is that six verses later, Ruth asked Boaz, a rich land owner, to perform a task that would change her life forever. To which he replied, *"I will do to thee all that thou require..."* And he did. In the next chapter, Boaz makes an inquiry of a near-kinsman and is ultimately granted the desire of *his* petition. [24]

As gold can only bond with gold, the Prayer of Agreement bonds us to the faith of others who have *like precious faith.* Consider the following:

- Ruth walked in agreement with Naomi.
- That propelled Boaz to walk in agreement with Ruth.
- The next of kin yielded to Boaz.
- Ruth and Boaz agreed with Naomi and married.
- This flow of agreement produced a great grandson: King David.

If Jesus is perfect theology—and He is, we can follow *His* faith. Prior to turning water into wine, Jesus *had not passed that way before.* He was then compelled to follow the faith of the voice that God had placed in His life (His mother's). Unity was needed to release the commanded blessing. So, when His mother asked Him to address the lack of wine issue, Jesus, fighting unbelief, had to follow her faith. And by walking in agreement with His mother's faith in Him, He was able to perform the first miracle of His ministry.

Walking in agreement is not without its battles:

- Peter fought *doubt* to follow Jesus' faith saying, *"...nevertheless at thy Word I will let down the net."*
- Esther fought *fear* to follow Mordecai's faith, even at the risk of losing her life, saying, *"...if I perish, I perish"* (Esther 4:16).
- Jesus, fighting *unbelief*, told the servants, *"... Fill the waterpots with water"* (John 2:7).

- Ruth, fighting *poverty*, followed Naomi's faith, saying, *"All that thou says unto me I will do."*

It appears that walking in agreement releases the commanded blessing on our lives, as well as a generational blessing. In essence, each person was connected to the faith of another's perspective; not their own. The Prayer of Agreement also focuses on the concept of harmony. Where brethren walk in unity, there God has commanded the blessing.

Jehovah Shammah
The Lord is There

Ezekiel 48:35

This Redemptive Name promises us that God, being our Lord, will never leave us, forsake us, nor fail us. He will never give up on us; we can count on His abiding presence to be with us, always. In Exodus 33:14, God promised Moses saying, *"My Presence shall go with you, and I will give you rest."* With the power of this name, His presence becomes our dwelling place; exclaiming, "The Glory has returned!"

Jehovah Shammah was there for Joseph:

Consider the patriarch, Joseph. He was aware of who he was and whose he was. Yet, he found himself in the midst of trouble. Acts 7:9-10 says: *"And the patriarchs, moved with envy, sold Joseph into Egypt: but God was with him, and delivered him out of all his afflictions..."* He was hated by his brothers, thrown into a waterless pit, sold as a slave, lied on, and put into prison; virtually forgotten. But the Bible says: *"And the Lord was with Joseph, and he was a prosperous man...And his master saw that the Lord was with him, and that the Lord made all that he did to prosper in his hand."* [25]

The Lord turned what the enemy meant for evil, for good—for both Joseph and his family—he provided food for them in the midst of a famine.

Joseph proved that the storms of life will come, but when God is with you, the charges levied against you are no match for God's love.

Jehovah Shammah was there for Moses:

As a child, Moses' life had been threatened. The pharaoh charged all his people to cast into the river, every son born to the children of Israel. But Jehovah Shammah was there for Moses. His parents hid him for three months because they saw that he was a *proper child*, and were not afraid of the king's commandment.[26] With this act, his parents operated in the Process of Discernment Agreement and Moses' life was supernaturally spared. This act not only saved his life, but a nation was also delivered from bondage.

Jehovah Shammah was there for Mephibosheth:

When Jonathan, the son of King Saul, was killed in battle, King David asked his men to find any living heir of his covenant friend, Jonathan. They found a young man by the name of Mephibosheth. Although he was lame in both feet and living in a place called Lo-debar, King David showed him the kindness of the Lord. He allowed Mephibosheth to sit and eat at his table as one of his own sons.[27] Jehovah Shammah sent Mephibosheth help from the sanctuary.

Jehovah Shammah makes us more than conquerors.

Jehovah Shammah
Promises Kept in His Name

❖ Because the Lord is there: *"...there was not one city too strong for us: the* LORD *our God delivered all unto us"* (Deuteronomy 2:36).

❖ Because the Lord is there: *"There shall no evil befall thee, neither shall any plague come nigh thy dwelling"* (Psalms 91:10).

❖ Because the Lord is there: *"And the water covered their enemies: there was not one of them left"* (Psalms 106:11).

❖ Because the Lord is there: *"There shall no evil happen to the just: but the wicked shall be filled with mischief"* (Proverbs 12:21).

❖ Because the Lord is there: *"There are many devices in a man's heart; nevertheless the counsel of the Lord, that shall stand"* (Proverbs 19:21).

❖ Because the Lord is there: *"There is no fear in love; but perfect love cast out fear: because fear has torment. He that fears is not made perfect in love"* (1 John 4:18).

❖ Because the Lord is there: *"...no man should be moved by these afflictions: for yourselves know that we are appointed thereunto"* (1 Thessalonians 3:3).

Call to Action:

1. Declare that you are no longer a child tossed to a fro by every wind of doctrine.

2. *"And have put on the new man, which is renewed in knowledge after the image of him that created him"* (Colossians 3:10).

3. Ask the Father to give you the wisdom to discern good and bad.

Pray:
That the Lord give you understanding in all things.
(2 Timothy 2:7)

Confess:
I am the head and not the tail.

Chapter 1

1. Ecclesiastes 10:16-17
2. Galatians 4:1
3. Ephesians 4:14
4. 2 Corinthians 6:14-18
5. Hebrews 4:16
6. John 1:12
7. Luke 2:52
8. 2 Peter 3:18
9. Isaiah 58:11
10. 1 John 2:20
11. Luke 3:22
12. Jeremiah 22:3
13. Luke 11:13
14. Numbers 23:20
15. Romans 3:21-22
16. Romans 8:1-2
17. 1 Kings 3:16-28
18. Amos 3:3;
19. Mark 3:25
20. Luke 5:5
21. Esther 2:25
22. Esther 2:20
23. Esther 1:12-22
24. Ruth 3:5; 3:11; 4
25. Genesis 39:2-3
26. Hebrews 11:23
27. 2 Samuel 9

Thy kingdom come.

Chapter 2

Deliverance through Feeding the Hungry Soul

Thy kingdom come, evokes the Prayer of Commitment—the casting of care; even legitimate care. Through this prayer we call on Jehovah Rohi - the Lord our Shepherd, to restore the soul. The strategy for this petition addresses the need to *feed the hungry soul.* Operating the Process of Overcoming, we are instructed to buy the truth.

A young woman was complaining about being rejected by her mother. I asked the Holy Spirit for a word of knowledge. I wanted Him to reveal the root cause of her feelings. God said, "Jealousy." So, I imparted this wisdom to her, but she rejected it immediately, saying, "I'm not jealous of anyone."

Knowing that I had heard from God, I became bold in my assertion, saying, "Yes, the real issue is jealousy." As she protested the information, I was led to look up the definition in a Bible dictionary. It defined jealousy as: *The uneasiness which arises from the fear that another does or will enjoy some advantage which we desire for ourselves.* [1]

She was immediately convicted, saying, "I have never heard that before." She then began to laugh. Hearing the truth had set her free. Her limited perception (definition) of jealousy had held her soul in bondage, so that the Kingdom of God could not come. Her hungry soul also caused her to be out of step with her spirit.

The Hindrance to the Petition
(Hungry Soul)

We miss it on this level when we fail to minister to our hungry souls. The soul, being the expressive part of our being, cries out for deliverance. In the 25th chapter of Matthew, Jesus addressed His concern relative to the hungry soul: *"For I was an hungred, and ye gave me no meat: I was thirsty, and ye gave me no drink: I was a stranger, and ye took me not in: naked, and ye clothed me not: sick, and in prison, and ye visited me not"*

This soul had been sorely neglected. It found itself going through much tribulation, but there was no one to confirm it or to minister to it. And, when we do *not* minister to the soul, we are *called cursed* and *named goats*. The Bible says: *"And these shall go away into everlasting punishment: but the righteous into life eternal."*

Without faith, the soul tends to focus on the thoughts and opinions of the wicked one. And seeing no way out, it becomes much discouraged.[2] Rather than magnifying the Lord, it will magnify the problem—making a mountain out of a molehill. For this reason, we are called to examine ourselves, [3] to see if we are in the faith.

In the last days, perilous times will come; [4] not owing to the economy or any outside circumstances. Instead, the Bible says it will be for many reasons. The first listed is self-love—a focus on the flesh to the neglect of the soul. When we are not contending for the faith, our souls suffer. Being unable to rest on the promises of God, it cannot enter into the kingdom of God. Being out of alignment with the spirit, it becomes scattered and divided. And woe to a house divided—it cannot stand—contempt rules, as each aspect of our soul (emotions, intellect, imagination, mind, and will) is attacked:

The emotional attack—the secret weapon of the flesh:

Symptom: led by own emotions (2 Corinthians 6:12)
Cause: unequally yoked to unbelief
Result: free, yet enslaved

In many cities in the United States, people of color celebrate a holiday called Juneteenth in honor of the signing of the Emancipation Proclamation. What is unusual about this date is the fact that it is not the actual date that the Emancipation Proclamation was signed (January, 1862). Rather, in Texas, it was two years later before the slaves got the news. For those two years they were free, yet still enslaved.

Many of us experience this same phenomenon as it pertains to our liberty in Christ—we are free, yet still enslaved. Ephesians 2 speaks of how God has broken down the middle wall of partition between He and us. He has also abolished, in His flesh, the reasons for opposition. Yet, through our emotions, we still oppose God.

Although the Bible says every man shall bear rule in his *own house*, our emotions still rule many of us. And when we can't control our emotions, we are like a city broken down without walls: defenseless; with no fruit of temperance. Without self-control, our <u>soul</u> yields to the ungodly doctrine of unbelief. Traditional morals and restraints are abandoned, and common sense is rejected. We proceed to blame others.

In 2 Corinthians 6, Paul addressed this issue, stressing that the people were not in anguish because of *him*. Rather, they were distressed by their own bowels (affections and emotions). In other words, their emotions ruined their peaceful dispositions and prevented them from guarding their hearts to preserve the issues of life.

The solution, according to Paul, is to not be unequally yoked with unbelief. Unbelief is not only believing something God did not say, but it is also an exchange of thoughts: God's thoughts for flesh thoughts. It is an inner-man conflict. We are called to come out from among them, and be ye separate, and God will receive us as sons and daughters. We are not to touch and agree with negative emotions; this inner battle of unbelief can cause the loss of lives.

Absalom was the son of King David, who the Bible said: *"In all Israel, there was none so praised as Absalom, for his beauty."* Nevertheless, he was a young man driven by strong feelings; restricted by his own emotions.

When his brother violated his sister, Absalom took matters into his own hands and had him killed—he didn't agree with King David's handling of the situation. When Joab, David's captain, failed to respond to Absalom's second request, he had his field set on fire. Then, in preparation for taking the kingdom from King David, using his charm, the Bible said that he stole the hearts of the men of Israel.

Eventually, Absalom decided to take over the kingdom. King David realized what was going on, feared for his life, and was forced to flee Jerusalem because of the treason. The fact that David was King did not matter, and the fact that David was his father did not matter. When emotions rule, they are all that matters. They are king, they are father, and they are God. And when they are mixed with unbelief, they are also dangerous.

In the process of taking over his father's kingdom, the Bible says that Absalom rode upon a mule, and the <u>mule</u> went under an oak tree. Absalom was hung up on a branch and later killed. (2 Samuel 13-18)

The Bible is telling us that out of control emotions are akin to a dumb animal leading us in a way that seems right but ends in death. Negative emotions, according to scientists, can also damage our DNA. Left unchecked, they hinder our walk with God.

The intellect attack:

Symptom: decree unrighteous decrees (Isaiah 10)
Cause: judging after the sight of the eyes
Result: woe, a sorrow and trouble-filled life

When the intellect is attacked, it causes us to mislabel God's children; both the widow and the fatherless. In Isaiah 10, the culprits received a woe: a sorrow and a trouble-filled life. The Bible says it was because they decreed unrighteous decrees and wrote grievousness, which they then prescribed. These decrees were not in agreement with the kingdom of God, for such decrees deprived the needy of justice and robbed the poor of their rights. And, because of mislabeling they had no redress.

The enemy, aware that the decrees were unrighteous, said, *"...my hand has found as a nest the riches of the people: and as one gathers eggs that are left, have I gathered all the earth; and there was none that moved the wing, or opened the mouth, or peeped."* The enemy saw that there was no one executing justice and judgment against these unrighteous decrees; there was no intercession taking place that would allow God's will be done in earth as it is in heaven.

When Eve found herself desiring to be wise, she knew something was missing—there was a disconnect. Without God's intervention, she would have remained in that *mislabeled* state; never realizing her true identity: that she was, indeed, made in the image of God.

A young girl was having difficulty reading. Others of her age had passed her by, but she struggled. There were also other signs of academic shortfalls, as well. The Holy Spirit led me to research teaching processes. I discovered that in our culture we say: "Sally can't draw," whereas in other cultures they say: "Sally has not been taught to draw." I began adapting this teaching concept. With regular prayer, within three weeks this young girl was reading well. Her self-esteem was also restored.

When decisions are made without the spirit's involvement, we run the risk of decreeing unrighteous decrees. Isaiah 11, cautions us in this area, saying: "... *and he shall not judge after the sight of his eyes, neither reprove after the hearing of his ears: But with righteousness shall he judge the poor, and reprove with equity for the meek of the earth: and he shall smite the earth with the rod of his mouth, and with the breath of his lips shall he slay the wicked. And righteousness shall be the girdle of his loins, and faithfulness the girdle of his reins*" (Isaiah 11:2-5).

The imagination attack:

Symptom: scattered (Luke 1:51; Psalms 2:3)
Cause: vain imagination - pride
Result: we get off course

When the imagination is attacked, it causes us to imagine vain things. Prior to this test, we were <u>guarding</u> our hearts. So, the enemy says, *"Let us break their bands asunder, and cast away their cords from us* [free us from their guard]." The enemy is seeking a means of getting us off course; with the temptation of *pride*, he secures his plan.

In 2 Samuel 2:14-23, Asahel, the brother of Joab (David's captain), fell prey to a vain imagination. He acted on private logic. During a type of sparring match between Joab's army and Abner's, Asahel decided to match his skills against General Abner, rather than compete with a soldier of his own rank. The Bible says that he was light of foot as a wild roe, so he imaged that his skills would be equal to that of the general. Being a gazelle in the wild, all he lacked was an opportunity and Abner's armour would be a great spoil for him. Although Abner begged him to turn aside, twice, Asahel would not be persuaded. Finally Abner turned and smote him (with his spear) under the fifth rib and he died.

Asahel walked in the imagination of his own heart; without spiritual discernment. The *proud*, the Bible says, are scattered in the imagination of their own hearts. Once they enter into the temptation, they will not listen to reason. 2 Corinthians 10:4 exhorts us to cast down vain imaginations. When they are not cast down, our foolish hearts become darkened. It appears that vain imaginations are common-place when we are lured into the *field*—a dangerous place to be. We tend to resort to our animal nature. In the field, we become easily subject to the temptation of the flesh.

The mind attack—our thought processes:

Symptom: taking thoughts indiscriminately (Proverbs 23:7)
Cause: unrenewed mind - pride
Result: conformed to this world

Physically speaking, we may arrive at our destinations by foot, by car, by bus, or by plane. But in the spiritual realm, we arrive at our destinations by *thoughts*. For, as a man thinks in his heart so is he. Eat and drink the enemy says to us, but his heart is not with us—it's a setup.

In 2 Kings 5, the story is told about a man named Naaman. The Bible says he was a mighty man of valor, but he was a leper. Following the advice of a servant girl, the king of Syria sent Naaman to the king of Israel to be recovered of his leprosy. He was eventually sent to the prophet Elisha, who gave him the instructions that he had received from God.

The problem was that Naaman had some *thoughts* of his own. Following his mind, he *thought* that the cure would occur by a wave of the hand and a few words spoken over him. In order to walk in faith, he would have to take his thoughts captive and take *God's* thoughts. But, God's wisdom seemed foolish to him. So Naaman became offended. Finally, with the help of his servant, Naaman was fully persuaded. He then sold his pride, stopped listening to himself, submitted to the wisdom of God, and was clean.

Satan can't cast out Satan; Naaman's own mind had deceived him. The way *he thought* he would be delivered was not the way that he was delivered. Also, Naaman's way would not have cleansed him of his pride: the root cause of his condition. Humility did. We operate in humility when our thoughts line up with God's. To get God's thoughts, we must renew the mind (address the flesh). And, this is done through godly wisdom, not our own.

The will attack:

Symptom: unwillingness (Isaiah 1:19)
Cause: pleasant knowledge; sowing to the flesh
Result: can't eat the good of the land

Prior to qualifying for the Olympics, tryouts are required. In the spiritual realm, this is akin to having a willing mind. But when the will is under attack, you will disqualify yourself by not even showing up for the tryouts. The enemy pits your desire to do God's will against a desire of pleasant knowledge. According to Paul, to will was present but the performance of the good was not.

This is how Mordecai, in the Book of Esther, knew that Esther, upon the first request to go before the king on behalf of her people, was not a willing candidate. Her will was under attack. She used what we call <u>legitimate cares</u> to excuse her lack of will power, saying, in effect: There is but one law, and that is death, if I show up before the king without being invited. Nevertheless, with the help of Mordecai, Esther realized that even legitimate cares have to bow the knee to the will of God. Mordecai helped her to free her will and to at least show up for the tryouts—he taught her to not disqualify herself. Casting her care, Esther's will was released and she was able to fulfill the call of God on her life.

Esther learned a valuable lesson: Faith does not disqualify itself. It shows up for the tryouts. It turned out that the 'light' that was in Esther, reminding her of the threat of death, was actually darkness. It was the flesh, using legitimate cares, in an attempt to exert its will over her will to thwart the will of God. In Luke11:35, Jesus warns: *"Take heed therefore that the light which is in thee be not darkness."* To not miss God, we are called to *prove all things* (get our will in line with His will*)*. Show a readiness to use our will.

With the burning bush, Moses used his will, saying, *"I will now turn aside, and see this great sight, why the bush is not burnt. When the Lord saw that he turned aside to see, God called unto him out of the midst of the bush, and said, Moses, Moses. And he said, Here am I."* (Exodus 3) The willing and obedient eat the good of the land.

See if you qualify... show up for the tryouts.

The Strategy to Escape the Hindrance
(Feeding the Hungry Soul)

This strategy begins with acknowledging the three-fold nature of man: spirit, soul, and body. The spirit, made in the image of God, carries God's image, nature, and ability. The soul functions in God's likeness, giving us the means to think on God's level. The soul houses our mind, will, emotions, imaginations, and intellect. The body, being the temple of the Holy Spirit, allows us to contact the natural realm. It is your earth suit, but it is *not* the real you; your spirit is.

The spirit:

It is the spirit (heart) that is inditing (proclaiming) a good matter; 5 it is not afraid of evil tidings. The heart is fixed, trusting in the Lord. The heart is established, 6 and knowing the end from the beginning, it is serving the Lord with joyfulness and gladness of heart, for the abundance of things to come.7 It is *not* in agreement with the thoughts of a cast down soul. From the perspective of the spirit—seeing eye-to-eye with God—all is well!

Nevertheless, the wicked one, seeing the fixed heart, is grieved, knowing that his desire shall perish. Our charge is to walk in agreement with the spirit, as it focuses on the good report, only. This assignment is fulfilled as we seek first the kingdom of God and His righteousness. And all these things (that the spirit sees) will be added. 8

In 2 Kings 4:8-37, a couple's son died, but the wife refused to acknowledge anything but what was in her spirit. When her husband questioned her, she replied, *"It shall be well."* When questioned again by Elisha's servant, her response was, *"It is well."* And needless to say, it *was* well with her. The prophet was able to return her son back to her, alive.

The soul:

Unlike the spirit, the soul is *not* fixed. It must be saved. It takes time for the soul to walk in agreement with the spirit. A prophet of old described the process: The Kingdom of God is generated in the soul by the Word of Life, under the influence of the Holy Spirit. It is first, very small; there is only a blade, but it is full of promise; then the ear; then the full corn in the ear...the soul is then purified from all unrighteousness and can then partake of God's divine nature.[9] This concept speaks to the process of *seedtime and harvest.*

Consequently, the soul cannot be hurried; it must be given due process. Luke 21:19 says, it is through patience that we possess our souls. The soul *does* need to be edified; afterwards, it must be allowed to hope and quietly wait for the salvation of the Lord.[10] And we call this, *due season.*

Establishing the soul:

In Acts 14:22, Paul found himself: *"Confirming the souls of the disciples, and exhorting them to continue in the faith, and that we must through much tribulation enter into the kingdom of God."* The hungry soul cries out for its salvation: healing, deliverance, protection, blessing, and prosperity. Jesus demonstrated the importance of soul prosperity on the cross—where there were two thieves—one on His right side and one on His left side.[11] (From time to time we also find ourselves in one of these two positions.) The thief on the right *turned* to Jesus for the expressed purpose of feeding his hungry soul. The thief on the left had the same opportunity, but he chose to take the low road; he stayed in the flesh and received his just condemnation.

Although Jesus was bound, the Word of God within Him was not. He spoke words that healed the thief's (on the right) hurting soul, telling him, *"Today you will be with me in paradise."* [12] When the thief mixed those words with faith, he received rest for his soul.

You could say that 'paradise' is a type of rest for souls who believe. The thief on the left, representing the body/flesh, where things of God are foolish to the natural man, failed to minister to his soul and was cursed.

Feeding the hungry soul:

Again, the soul houses our will, mind, imagination, intellect, and emotions. Being formed, it can easily be *conformed* to the dictates of this world, *if* the mind is not *transformed*.

Interestingly, in the Bible, those who fed their hungry souls were named *blessed* and called *brethren*; they had a relationship with the Father. They lived under the covenant of promise, not alienated from it:

- When hungry, the *righteous* fed their hungry souls the Word of Life.
- When thirsty, they fed their faith.
- As a stranger, they worked their covenant.
- When naked, they clothed themselves with the fruit of the Spirit.
- When sick and in prison, they ministered unto the Lord; endured to the end; received the end of their faith; even the salvation of their souls with joy unspeakable. [13]

They were able to save their souls by taking the engrafted Word [14] and receiving it with the fruit of meekness. They purified their souls by being hearers and doers of the Word.

The role of the fruit of the Spirit:

Luke 13:6-9, tells the story of a man who had planted a fig tree in his vineyard; then came and sought fruit and found none. He addressed the dresser of the vineyard, telling him of plans to cut it down. The dresser explained that the tree just needed fertilizing. If it does not respond after that, then it shall be cut down.

Here, God is expressing the urgency of the need for fruit to restore the soul. John the Baptist explained that fruit was needed against an axe that was laid against the root of the tree. [15] Without fruit we cannot thwart the plan of the enemy. The soul without its fruit is under siege.

God gives us time to dress the *heart* and guard it. He is looking for the fruit of the Spirit: love, joy, peace, patience, kindness, goodness, faith, meekness, and temperance. This allows God to lead and guide us. Since we are only as strong as our weakest link, without some restraints against our carnal nature, we will be castaways (cut down).

The fruit of the Spirit is our only defense against what the Bible calls the wicked counselor; [16] known to us as the *flesh*. The fruit serves as a refuge against its fiery darts. When the fruit is present, the soul is guarded and the wicked has no recourse.

In the Song of Solomon, the bride requests the bridegroom to come into my garden and eat my precious fruit. [17] This is the cry of all of our *hearts*:

- We cry out for the fruit of Love to cover our sins.
- We cry out for the fruit of Joy to see the end of our faith.
- We cry out for the fruit of Peace to guard our hearts.
- We cry out for the fruit of Patience to possess our souls.
- We cry out for the fruit of Kindness to purify our souls.
- We cry out for the fruit of Goodness to lead us to repentance.
- We cry out for the fruit of Faith to please God.
- We cry out for the fruit of Meekness to guard against pride.
- We cry out for the fruit of Temperance to buffet our bodies.

John 15:8 says fruit-bearing is the proof of discipleship: *"Herein is my father glorified, that you bear much fruit; so shall you be my disciples."* The fruit we bear helps us to love our neighbor as we love ourselves.

My mother tells the story of how once, when she was in a state of uproar, she found herself giving the offending person a *piece of her mind.* But because she was met with kindness, she herself repented and asked for forgiveness.

The longing soul:

The soul longs, faints, cries, and wanders for the salvation of the Lord: *"My soul longeth, yea, even faints for the courts of the Lord: my heart and my flesh crieth out for the living God"* (Psalms 84:2).

"My soul fainteth for thy salvation: but I hope in thy word. Mine eyes fail for thy word, saying, When wilt thou comfort me" (Psalms 119:81-82).

"They wandered in the wilderness in a solitary way; they found no city to dwell in. Hungry and thirsty, their soul fainted in them" (Psalms 107:4-5).

The Process of Overcoming
Buying and Selling

(Guarding Your Soul)

This process focuses on restoring the soul; it provides the means for keeping the soul in alignment with the spirit.

Proverbs 23:23
- Wisdom (what): *"Buy the truth,*
- Understanding (why): *and sell it not*
- Knowledge (how): *also wisdom, and instruction, and understanding."*

Matthew 13:44 says: *"Again, the kingdom of heaven is like unto treasure hid in a field; the which when a man hath found, he hideth, and for joy thereof goeth and selleth all that he hath, and buyeth that field."*

Here, Jesus is sharing a parable relative to buying and selling. Good and evil cannot co-exist; it is akin to serving two masters. In order to buy into the wisdom of the treasure, you must dispossess squatters. For most of us, this may involve buying faith and selling doubt. It is through this process that we overcome, to restore the soul.

In 1 Samuel 25, the story is told of a man by the name of Nabal and of his wife, Abigail. She was a woman of good understanding, but her husband was churlish. David and his men, on their own, offered unsolicited protection for Nabal's men and his sheep. But when David sent messengers to ask for food for him and his men, Nabal said, *"Who is David... Shall I then take my bread, and my water, and my flesh that I have killed for my shearers, and give it unto men, whom I know not whence they be?"*

Upon hearing this, David then felt that Nabal had requited him evil for good, and he sought revenge. But Abigail gathered goods and went and met David and reasoned with him. She told him that folly is with her husband and that basically he (David) had a future to consider. David bought into her words of wisdom, received the supply of goods, and overcame his anger. He bought the truth and his soul was set free. David praised Abigail for her wisdom and for restraining him from avenging himself.

Thy Kingdom Come

Key elements of this petition:

The kingdom refers to God's dominion reign of righteousness, peace, and joy in the Holy Ghost: righteousness to bring our souls out of trouble, peace to safeguard the soul, and joy to clothe the soul.

The Hindrance to this petition lies in a hungry soul; to the hungry soul bitter things are sweet. A hungry man has no discretion; he will eat anything. He will succumb to one of three things that promise liberty, yet binds him: lust of the flesh, lust of the eyes, and the pride of life.

The Strategy calls for us to prosper our souls and be in health, even as our souls prosper. As you prosper your soul, you prosper your kingdom. (3 John 1:2)

Through the Process of Overcoming, we break unequal yokes from off our necks and bear rule in our own house. Buying the truth breaks the yoke and prospers the soul.

Thy kingdom come, cries out for fruitfulness to be manifested in our lives; giving the Prayer of Commitment the power to establish us; being empowered by Jehovah Rohi - the Lord, our Shepherd.

The Prayer of Commitment

This prayer calls for us to cast all of our care, including legitimate care, on Him—as explained in 1 Peter 5:5-9:

- Wisdom (what): *"Likewise, ye younger, submit yourselves unto the elder. Yea, all of you be subject one to another, and be clothed with humility:*
- Understanding (why): *for God resisteth the proud, and giveth grace to the humble."*

- Wisdom (what): *"Humble yourselves therefore under the mighty hand of* God,
- Understanding (why): *that he may exalt you in due time:*
- Knowledge (how): *Casting all your <u>care</u> upon him; for he careth for you."*

- Wisdom (what): *"Be sober, be vigilant;*
- Understanding (why): *because your adversary the devil, as a roaring lion, walketh about, seeking whom he may devour:*
- Knowledge (how): *Whom resist stedfast in the faith, knowing that the same afflictions are accomplished in your brethren that are in the world."*

Here, the proud and the humble are being contrasted. The proud are those with care; these individuals are being resisted, not helped by God. The humble (those who cast their care) are given grace, and in due season they will be exalted. According to 1 Peter 5, the devil is seeking whom he may devour, and he can *only* devour those with care.

The story of Achan, in the book of Joshua, [18] shows the destructive power of *care*. Joshua and the children of Israel had no problem defeating Jericho with its walled-city. Therefore, when it was time for the second battle, they assumed the little town of Ai would be even easier to conquer. Yet, they were defeated. After inquiring why, God told them that someone had transgressed His commandment; that until this was addressed, they would not be able to stand before their enemies. And also, that God Himself would not be among them.

They discovered that the transgressor was a man by the name of Achan. This man, instead of hiding the Word of God in his heart, had hidden the enemy's goods in his heart—things that he cared about. His care brought about a defeat for them all. The Israelites could not overcome the enemy without until they defeated the enemy of care, within.

In Song of Solomon, *care* is known as the *little* foxes that spoil the vine. [19] In the New Testament, it the *little* leaven that leavens the whole lump. [20] Jesus also identified the cares of this world as one of the factors that made the Word of God unfruitful. [21] Whether cares are called concerns, anxiety, pet-peeves, irritants, or even what we call legitimate cares, they will make you unable to stand before your enemies.

Mercy triumphs over judgment:

Our heavenly Father is looking for agreement; so is the devil. The devil is searching for fears, cares, doubt, unbelief, and strong desires. He is looking for agreement relative to the state of your failing health, the welfare of your loved ones, or any negative state of being.

He also wants you to lay your hands on the prey (those who are being used by the devil to draw you into the natural arena). He is endeavoring to keep you focused on your circumstances: See the lack. See the need. See the fault. See the problem.

Recently I encountered a situation where I was faced with who the Bible calls 'an accuser of the brethren.' [22] After the interaction, I was bombarded by thoughts of how unfairly I was treated. My care was the distress of being misunderstood. In situations of this nature, the *enemy* is calling for the rendering of judgment; even questioning the sincerity of the offender's faith. But

1 Peter 5:7 says when faced with care, we are to cast the care and remain stedfast in the faith. And when in faith, mercy triumphs over judgment.[23] So, I chose not to focus on the prey; instead, I came against the enemy that was behind the attack (the devil). I took captive every thought.

Afterwards, the Holy Spirit told me to go forward, and then He asked what grade I would give myself for my course of action.

I said, "An A."

Then He said, "No, an A plus."

I asked, "Why an A plus?"

He said, "Because you took no account of evil done to you, and you paid no attention to a suffered wrong."

Care will cause us to speak out of a faulty perception. The Prayer of Commitment calls for us to be sober and vigilant. We should have a sword ready to quench every fiery dart of the wicked. We choose mercy over judgment—we *choose* to feed the hungry soul.

Feeding the enemy:

We are not to take matters into our own hands. Vengeance is mine says the Lord. Because the offender is hungry, Romans 12 says he is to be fed. *If they enemy is hungry, feed him. If thirsty, give him drink.* In 2 Kings 5, although a little servant girl had been taken captive by Naaman, she gave him knowledge that would recover him of his leprosy. She punished his flesh. Then was Naaman's flesh clean, and he pledged to serve God.

Jehovah Rohi – the Lord our Shepherd

Psalms 23

As the Shepherd of our souls, the Lord leads us, guides us, and restores our souls. Because the soul is prone to wander, it must be dressed and guarded, suggesting that fruit is needed to stabilize it.

Jehovah Rohi was there for Jonah:

Jonah found himself in a situation where his soul fainted within him, but he used the voice of thanksgiving and was delivered: *"When my soul fainted within me I remembered the LORD: and my prayer came in unto thee, into thine holy temple... But I will sacrifice unto thee with the voice of thanksgiving... And the LORD spake unto the fish, and it vomited out Jonah upon the dry land"* (Jonah 2:7-10).

Jehovah Rohi was there for David:

"And David was greatly distressed; for the people spake of stoning him, because the soul of all the people was grieved, every man for his sons and for his daughters: but, David encouraged himself in the LORD his God" (1 Samuel 30:6-19). David said, *"Why art thou cast down, O my soul? And why art thou disquieted in me? Hope thou in God: for I shall yet praise him for the help of his countenance"* (Psalms 42:5).

What's interesting is that David's mighty men considered the use of natural means (stone him) when their souls were grieved. But David, turned to the Shepherd of his soul. God gave him an instruction: *Pursue: for thou shall surely overtake them, and without fail recover all.* Then David sold his distress and bought the truth. With this act, he operated in the Process of Overcoming. The Bible says: *"David recovered all."*

49

Jehovah Rohi
Promises Kept in His Name

❖ As our Shepherd, *"For he satisfieth the longing soul and fills the hungry soul with goodness"* (Psalms 107:9).

❖ As our Shepherd, *"My soul, wait thou only upon God; for my expectation is from him"* (Psalms 62:5).

❖ As our Shepherd, *"Deliver my soul, O Lord, from lying lips, and from a deceitful tongue"* (Psalms 120:2).

❖ As our Shepherd, *"The Lord shall preserve thee from all evil: he shall preserve thy soul"* (Psalms 121:7).

❖ As our Shepherd, *"Our soul is escaped as a bird out of the snare of the fowlers: the snare is broken, and we are escaped"* (Psalm 124:7).

❖ As our Shepherd, *"And the LORD shall guide thee continually, and satisfy thy soul in drought, and make fat thy bones: and thou shalt be like a watered garden, and like a spring of water, whose waters fail not"* (Isaiah 58:11).

Call to Action:

1. Cast all of your care and legitimate care on Him.

2. *"But let us, who are of the day, be sober, putting on the breastplate of faith and love; and for an helmet, the hope of salvation"* (1 Thessalonians 5:8).

3. Encourage yourself in the Lord.

Pray:
"...that ye may stand perfect and complete in all the will of God" (Colossians 4:12).

Confess:
God satisfies my soul in drought. (Isaiah 58:11)

Chapter 2

1. Webster's 1828 Dictionary
2. Numbers 21:4
3. 2 Corinthians 13:5
4. 2 Timothy 3:1-5
5. Psalms 45:1
6. Psalms 112:7-10
7. Deuteronomy 28:47-48
8. Matthew 6:33
9. Adam Clarke-Internet Commentary/ Public Domain
10. Lamentations 3:26
11. Matthew 27:38
12. Luke 23:39-43
13. 1 Peter 1:9
14. James 1:21
15. Luke 3:9
16. Nahum 1:11
17. Song of Songs 4:16
18. Joshua 7
19. Song of Songs 2:15
20. 1 Corinthians 5:6
21. Mark 4:19
22. Revelation 12:10
23. James 2:13

Thy will be done in earth,
as it is in heaven.

Chapter 3

Deliverance through a Willing Mind

*T*hy will be done in earth, as it is in heaven, evokes the Prayer of Consecration—yielding our will to do God's will. Through this prayer, we call on Jehovah Tsidkenu – the Lord our Righteousness to direct all of our ways. The strategy for this petition addresses the alignment of the will—*the willing mind.* Operating the Process of Occupying, we start by maintaining a military presence against a doubtful mind.

I was asked to complete a task that was, in the natural, very difficult for me, but I knew that God was in it. Refusing to speak my doubt and unbelief, I acknowledged that the assignment was from God, although for months I could not see how it could be accomplished. And when the day came for the task to be started, all I could bring to the table was a *willing mind.*

To my amazement, I was able to rise to the occasion. First, I found myself laying the foundation; then week after week, God was there confirming His Word. Finally, the Holy Spirit gave me a Word; it came from Isaiah 40:2: *"...your warfare is accomplished."* I had *performed* the task that He had called me to do. When I gave God my will, He supplied the power to perform the task; however, not without a battle.

My initial perceptions told me that the task could not be done, and I found myself being a judge of evil thoughts, such as: *this can't happen; they don't know enough; it would take too long,* and like the children of Israel, I thought, *there are giants in the land.* But the sceptre of righteousness (of faith) had already been drawn: a willing mind!

A willing mind is a type of gatekeeper that lays the foundation for God's involvement. It involves going without knowing (Abraham's strategy); being single-minded (Ruth's strategy); fighting the flesh (Paul's strategy); then following the righteousness that is of faith.

The Hindrance to the Petition
(Doubtful Mind)

We often confess Jesus as Savior, even acknowledging His saving grace. But because of a doubtful mind, He is not always Lord. We miss it on this level when we fail to consider the input of the spirit man—who is always willing. Doubt often arises from *a defect of knowledge or evidence*. [1] Not fighting the doubt, we find ourselves wavering, being double-minded, unstable, and hypocritical.

Seeing the evidence of a bloody coat, Jacob, the father of Joseph, said, *"Without a doubt, an evil beast had devoured him."* Because of unbelief, he doubted that his son could still be alive. Doubt caused him to mourn for thirteen years, needlessly. Doubt manipulated his perception of reality; the reality being: Joseph was still alive. [2]

When the barbarians saw the venomous beast hang on Paul's hand, they said, *"No doubt, this man is a murderer."* And therefore vengeance suffered him not to live. Yet Paul, walking in his authority, shook the beast off into the fire and felt no harm.[3] In both cases they believed information that confirmed their manipulated perceptions, but they were in error.

It has been said that if you consider the right thing, it will feed your faith. But, if you consider the wrong thing, it will feed your unbelief. By taking anxious thoughts, we will find ourselves omitting the weightier matters, such as: judgment, mercy, and faith. [4] In the Bible, these individuals received a woe! They failed to render judgment against a doubtful mind. They were called hypocrites and named 'blind guides.'

This is what happened to King Saul. He was told to destroy the Amalekites, but he made the decision to save the best of the bounty as a sacrifice. As an act of his will, he chose to walk contrary to the will of God, and not by faith. He kept his own will and did what made sense to him. *God said: "It repented me that I have set up Saul to be king: for he is turned back from following me, and has not <u>performed</u> my commandments..."* (1 Samuel 15:11).

In Luke 1, the story is told of Zacharias and his wife, Elisabeth, the parents of John the Baptist. The Bible said *"...they were both righteous before God, walking in all the commandments and ordinances of the Lord blameless."* But, *"...Elisabeth was barren, and they both were now well stricken in years."*

As Zacharias executed the priest's office, an angel of the Lord met him, to tell him that his prayer was heard. And, that they shall have a child and shall call his name, John, and many shall rejoice at his birth; that he shall make ready a people prepared for the Lord.

Being overwhelmed by the prophesy, Zacharias said unto the angel, *"How shall I know this, I am an old man, and my wife well stricken in years."* Detecting doubt, the angel answered and said, *"I am Gabriel... and I'm sent to shew thee these glad tidings."*

Then, the angel proceeded to instruct Zacharias on how to deal with the doubt, *"And, behold, thou shall be dumb, and not able to speak until the day that these things shall be performed, because you believed not my words which shall be fulfilled in their season."*

The angel had to get the doubt out. In Isaiah 53:7, the Bible explained how Jesus dealt with doubt: *"He was oppressed, and he was afflicted, yet he opened not his mouth: he is brought as a lamb to the slaughter, and as a sheep before her shearers is dumb, so he openeth not his mouth."*

Although we are called to be boxers, some of us can't take a punch. We falter under the impact and speak out doubt and unbelief, to negatively affect the prophesy and due season. The wisdom, given by the angel, gave Zacharias the strength to endure till the end. Being righteous, Zacharias obeyed. Although oppressed, by the natural limitations, he did not speak the doubt.

When Elisabeth brought forth their son, and after Zacharias confirmed that his son's name was John: his mouth was opened, his tongue loosed, and he spake and praised God. Zacharias was then able to deliver the prophesy: *...That God would perform the mercy promised to our fathers and remember His holy covenant.* Doubt tried to stop the birth and the prophesy.

The Strategy to Escape the Hindrance
(A Willing Mind)

"Now therefore <u>perform the doing</u> of it; that as there was a <u>readiness to will</u>, so there may be <u>a performance</u> also out of that which ye have. For if there be <u>first a willing mind</u>, it is accepted according to that a man hath, and not according to that he hath not" (2 Corinthians 8:11-12).

Here, God is preparing us to be *doers* of the Word; He is searching for a 'readiness to will' so that we may *perform* the doing of it.

The prophet Elijah was commanded by God to go to the widow woman whom God had commanded to sustain him. [5] Upon arriving, he first asked the woman for a little water; she went to comply. Observing that she had a *readiness to will,* he then asked for a little bread. But because of the famine, the woman told Elijah that she only had a handful of meal and a little oil—just enough for her and her son to eat and die. Nevertheless, because she had already shown him a willing mind, Elijah knew that she was in faith.

Elijah then gave her a Word from the Lord, *"Make me a little cake first, and bring it unto me and after make for thee and for thy son. For thus said the Lord. The barrel of meal shall not waste; neither shall the cruse of oil fail, until the day that the Lord sends rain upon the earth."*

The Bible says she went and did according to the saying of Elijah, and she and he, and her house, did eat many days. The widow overcame her doubt, by a readiness to will. She was then in a position to receive the Word of God from the mouth of the prophet, and God was then able to supply the power to perform the task.

Notice that God, Himself, had not spoken to her. Some present day saints are quick to say, "God did not tell me!" But if the widow had maintained *that* posture, she and her son would have died. Faith requires first a willing mind. Parked cars are difficult to direct.

A willing mind calls for us to fight the *contradiction* (a contrary declaration). According to Proverbs, wise counsel makes war—6 the enemy will always come against the wisdom of God. If we are *not* willing to consider the spirit in the decisions that we face, we become blind guides. In the natural, the widow was limited; there was a famine. Spiritually however, she was willing. By overcoming doubt, she retained her will and her power. Neither the barrel of meal wasted , nor did the cruse of oil fail. Because she was willing, God was able to direct her—not directly, but indirectly.

In the New Testament, the woman with the issue of blood had a *readiness to will* also, but not before ignoring her mind—she simply refused to listen to her own mind. Then, being free to follow her spirit, she was ready to *perform* her faith: "*For she said within herself, If I <u>may</u> but touch his garment, I <u>shall</u> be whole*" (Matthew 9:21). Then, "*...came behind Him, and touched the border of His garment*" (Luke 8:44).

The Prodigal Son addressed his mind also. He came to himself, and said, "*I <u>will</u> arise and go to my father...And he arose, and came to his father*" (Luke 15:18-20).

After they fought the battle within, they followed up with corresponding actions. They followed their faith to perform the doing of it. Neither the woman with the issue of blood, nor the Prodigal Son disqualified or second-guessed himself. God is looking for those who have: "*...inclined their hearts to perform His statutes...so that He may perform the mercy promised to our fathers, and to remember His holy covenant.*"7 In Isaiah 44:28, God says of Cyrus, "*...He is my shepherd, and shall perform all my pleasure.*"

Our will establishes our hearts. The test of the willing mind says: He who has, more will be given. God is testing our capacity to carry a seed first; thus enabling Him to bring the increase.

Virtue released:

When God, our Father, tells us to take captive every thought, He wants us to guard our hearts from contaminating influences. The Bible says if there be any virtue or praise, we are to think on things that are: true, honest, just, pure, lovely, and of a good report. When thoughts are full of virtue— a good report, God's anointing can flow.

After being out in the hot sun, I didn't want to make another trip. Then the thought came to me: *Ask your husband to go for you.* Usually he doesn't want to go out in the traffic—so the next thought said: *You know he's going to say no.* I said: "I can't think that thought, there is no virtue in it. That's not a good report." So I asked him anyway, and he said, "Yes," without hesitation. A willing mind does not disqualify itself.

Keeping the will in the arena of faith, releases the true potential of the spirit as it indites a good matter.

The Process of Occupying
Hearing and Keeping

(Guarding Your Will)

This process involves the principle of occupying, where we are called to guard our will against the desires of the flesh by maintaining a military presence around the <u>crucified</u> flesh.

The Occupy Alert

Luke 19:13-26
- Wisdom (what): *"A certain nobleman went into a far country to receive for himself a kingdom, and to return. And he called his ten servants, and delivered them ten pounds, and said unto them, <u>Occupy till I come</u>. But his citizens hated him...He said unto them that stood by, Take from him the pound, and give it to him that has ten pounds.*
- Understanding (why): *And they said unto Him, Lord he has ten pounds.* [Because he guarded the instruction.]
- Knowledge (how): *For I say unto you, that unto everyone which has shall be given; and from him that has not, even that he has shall be taken away from him."*

God is trying to get something to us. To do so, we must guard the will. This is done by presenting our bodies as a living sacrifice. [8] The body must be free to follow the dictates of the spirit, not the mind. Instead, the mind is to be transformed by renewing it, for whatever thought that is not transformed will be transferred into unbelief by the unrenewed mind. A willing mind begins with fighting doubt in the heart and holding the beginning of our confidence steadfast to the end. It *guards* the seed of the instruction.

The body leads:

While picking up a friend, after ringing the door bell and returning to where I had parked, I found myself going around to the other side of the car. Although I was following the leading of my spirit, I was also wondering, *why am I going to this side of the car?* Then suddenly I saw a piece of mail on the ground that looked rather important, so I picked up the envelope. My friend had accidentally dropped it on her way from the mail box. She appreciated the find, proving that the letter was important.

We are to present our bodies, under the influence of the spirit, and renew the mind. Our minds are clueless. (Romans 12:1-2)

Thy Will Be Done in Earth, as it is in Heaven

Key elements of this petition:

The Hindrance to this petition lies in a failure to align our will to the will of God. This petition is covenant based: *if* we are willing and obedient, *then* we shall eat the good of the land. When the will is under attack, our desire is compromised and so is our power. One pastor warns that the flesh will even try to get us to do the will of God, *its* way: go to church, but don't lift up your hands; forgive but don't forget...in other words: don't go too far. Or, we may find ourselves saying, "I don't feel like it...I'm too tired... I don't want to." It's an attack against your will.

The Strategy calls for us to fight doubt by holding the beginning of our confidence steadfast till the end. (Hebrews 3:14)

Through the Process of Occupying, we hear the Word and keep it. We then become hearers and doers of the Word; prepared for the storms of life.

Thy will be done, as it is in heaven, calls for us to prioritize His will over the will of the flesh; thus giving the Prayer of Consecration the power to perform God's will in our lives; being empowered by Jehovah Tsidkenu - the Lord, our Righteousness.

The Prayer of Consecration

This prayer focuses on doing the will of God from the heart; it addresses the attack of doubt.

2 Corinthians 8:11-12

- Wisdom (what): *"Now therefore perform the doing of it; that as there was a readiness to will,*
- Understanding (why): *so there may be a performance also out of that which ye have.*
- Knowledge (how): *For if there be first a willing mind, it is accepted according to that a man hath, and not according to that he hath not."*

Paul was endeavoring to do the will of God; asserting that his delight was in the law of God after the inward man. Paul said the *will* was there but the *performance* was not. This, said Paul, was due to another law in his members, warring against the law of his mind; bringing him into captivity to the law of sin which was in his members. 9 The law in his members was evoking the righteousness of the *law*, while he was endeavoring to do the righteousness of *faith*.10 Paul realized that the flesh was asserting its undue influence in order to hinder the work of God in the earth.

The righteousness of the law can cause us to oppose the inner man; then we become partakers of evil thoughts.11 We find ourselves watching for infractions of the rules (law); holding self and others to the letter of the law, not grace. On the other hand, *thy will be done* employs the sceptre of righteousness by faith; especially the God kind of faith where we see things from God's point of view. This level of faith involves a sacrifice of our will.

First, God calls for a willing mind:

- For Abraham, a willing mind meant going without knowing: *"By faith Abraham, when he was called to go out into a place which he should after receive for an inheritance, obeyed; and he went out, not knowing whither he went"* (Hebrews 11:8).

- For Paul a willing mind meant keeping his mind on the things of God: *"For they that are after the flesh do mind the things of the flesh; but they that are after the Spirit the things of the Spirit"* (Romans 8:5).

- For Ruth a willing mind meant being steadfast-minded or even single-minded: *"When she saw that she was steadfastly minded to go with her, then she left speaking unto her"* (Ruth 1:18).

- For David a willing mind meant having God's agenda: *"...I have found David the son of Jesse, a man after mine own heart, which shall fulfil all my will"* (Acts 13:22).

- For Jesus, a willing mind meant watching and praying the Prayer of Consecration: *"Not my will, but thine be done."* [12]

For us, a willing mind means that in whatever circumstances we find ourselves, we must be willing to allow God to lead and guide us. Jeremiah 10:23 says, we cannot direct our own steps.

63

Jehovah Tsidkenu
The Lord - our Righteousness

Jeremiah 23:6

The Lord - our Righteousness protects against the forces of darkness joined against us. He leads us in the way we should go, and prepares us for the attack. In Isaiah 54, God says that He has seen the weapons formed against us by the enemy, even the tongue of judgment, but his weapons will not prosper. For this is the heritage of the servants of the Lord.

Jehovah Tsidkenu was there:

"Riches profit not in the day of wrath: but righteousness delivereth from death" (Proverbs 11:4).

A friend of mine shared the following testimony of how God led her in the way of righteousness—saving her son's life:

Years ago, I was considering cutting my tithes in half, because of unexpected bills/expenses. But I didn't feel right even thinking about it, so I sought the multitude of counsel (senior ministers in the church). They agreed that it would be ok, just a few times, to reduce my tithes. Nevertheless, when the time came for me to write out the check for tithing, I could not change (lessen) the amount that I usually wrote.

Shortly thereafter, my son came home and informed me that he had been in a terrible car accident; the car was totaled. I immediately asked, "So where is the car, and what did you hit?" He told me that the car had hydroplaned up a hill, spun 180 degrees, jumped the street curb, and hit a small tree.

It wasn't until I arrived at the scene of the accident that the magnitude of it hit me. I walked up to the car and saw that the driver's side door was indented by maybe a foot, the window was smashed in, the front wheel and axle were separated from the car, and the driver's seat was raised and touching the steering column.

And then it came: a vision of a very large hand! I immediately wept, giving God praise and thanking Him for saving my son's life.

The next morning, while doing my devotions, God led me to the promise of God that had been activated on my behalf: *"...righteousness delivers from death."* God led me into the path of righteousness, for his Name's sake.

What looked like a simple decision-making process was actually a battle for the life of her son. This mom remained steadfast in her giving. And with this act, she operated in the Process of Occupying.

Obeying the voice of your conscience:

Should I turn right or should I turn left? It is not a decision, it is a battle. Should I go here, or there? Again, it is not a decision, it is a battle. When the conscience is endeavoring to lead us in the path of righteousness, it is being opposed, and we are receiving another's influence (input)—the flesh's. The Bible says the spirit fights against the flesh and the flesh against the spirit. These are contrary the one to the other, so that we cannot do the things we ought. It is there opposing the good counsel of God. Notwithstanding, Jehovah Tsidkenu is also there directing our steps toward the path of righteousness.

To follow His lead, we must:
- immediately obey the voice of our conscience;
- the conscience cannot be answered;
- Only obeyed. If you answer it, you lose

—for you have placed yourself on equal par with God. You are now directing your own steps. You failed to fight the doubt.

Thought-intercept: fighting doubt

Obeying the voice of our conscience is necessary when we are confronted with an attack against our will. We must fight doubt. Doubt comes disguised as: fear, horror, dread, questions, being suspect, distrust, wavering, hesitating, being undetermined, and even defects of knowledge or evidence. [13]

A young man was studying for an exam. During this time, he was prompted by the voice of his conscience to study an item that was not listed on his prep sheet. Being <u>undetermined</u>, he answered it... saying to himself: *I don't think that is going to be on the test.* This prompting occurred twice. To the surprise of the whole class, that item was on the test. And, ignoring his conscience affected his grade. Our conscience cannot be answered, only obeyed.

This attack is called: thought-intercept. When the voice of our conscience is intercepted by another thought, we simply fight the doubt. Peter countered his intercepting thought with: Nevertheless, at thy Word, *I will...*

Righteousness delivers from reproach—condemnation:

An eagle's natural enemy is the raven. Although the eagle is much more regal, the raven likes to vex him. During these times, the eagle just flies higher. Our flesh is similar; it vexes us with condemnation: doubt, regret, belittlement, guilt, and confusion—endeavoring to take our crown. Revelation 3:11 warns us to hold fast that which we have, *"...that no man take thy crown."* Fight back. Job 27:6 says: *"My righteousness I hold fast. And I will not let it go: my heart shall not reproach me so long as I live."*

Righteousness is a gift that must be protected. You can't reign without it. Moreover, condemnation kills. When we miss it, we judge ourselves and then go forward. We fly higher.

Jehovah Tsidkenu
Promises Kept in His Name

❖ *"Fear thou not; for I am with thee: be not dismayed; for I am thy God: I will strengthen thee; yea, I will help thee; yea, I will uphold thee with the right hand of my righteousness"* (Isaiah 41:10).

❖ *"The LORD will not suffer the soul of the righteous to famish: but he casteth away the substance of the wicked"* (Proverbs 10:3).

❖ *"I the LORD have called thee in righteousness, and will hold thine hand, and will keep thee, and give thee for a covenant of the people, for a light of the Gentiles"* (Isaiah 42:6).

❖ *"And I will betroth thee unto me forever; yea, I will betroth thee unto me in righteousness, and in judgment, and in lovingkindness, and in mercies"* (Hosea 2:19).

❖ *"For I will be merciful to their unrighteousness, and their sins and their iniquities will I remember no more"* (Hebrews 8:12).

❖ *"My righteousness I hold fast, and will not let it go: my heart shall not reproach me so long as I live"* (Job 27:6).

❖ *"In righteousness shalt thou be established: thou shalt be far from oppression; for thou shalt not fear: and from terror; for it shall not come near thee"* (Isaiah 54:14).

Call to Action:

1. Purpose that you will not allow doubt or fear to interfere with the Father's plan for your life.

2. *"But put ye on the Lord Jesus Christ, and make not provision for the flesh, to fulfil the lusts thereof"* (Romans 13:14).

3. Ask the Father to guide you in renewing your mind to guard you against the desires of the flesh.

Pray:
That God is in all of your thoughts. (Psalms 10:4)

Confess:
I have been made the righteousness of God in Him.
(2 Corinthians 5:21)

Chapter 3

1. Webster's 1828 Dictionary
2. Genesis 37:33; 45:28
3. Acts 28:4-5
4. Matthew 23:23
5. 1 Kings 17:9-16
6. Proverbs 24:6
7. Luke 1:72
8 Romans 12:1-2
9. Romans 7:18-23
10. Romans 4:13; 10:5-6; Galatians 5:5
11. James 2:4
12. Luke 22:42
13. Webster's 1828 Dictionary

Give us this day our daily bread.

Chapter 4

Deliverance through Taming the Tongue

*G*ive us this day our daily bread, evokes the Prayer of Petition; sometimes called the Prayer of Faith. Through this prayer we call on Jehovah Jireh - the Lord our Provider to supply our needs. The strategy for this petition combats the daily attacks that we suffer because of an unruly tongue. Operating the Process of Effectual Prayer, we believe we receive.

I came in contact with a young lady who was seventeen years old. She had a great personality and was very warm-hearted—a people person. She wanted a job, so we prayed for favor. But time after time she came back to tell me that she had interviewed for a job but didn't get it. I was confounded; thinking, *anyone would hire her*. I couldn't figure out what the problem was. Finally, I asked her, "After you put in your application, what do you say to yourself?"

She responded, "I tell myself that they are *not* going to hire me." I then explained that her tongue was the issue. So, I put some order into her conversation:

"The next time you submit your application, say to yourself, *I will get this job*." She did, and not only did she get that job, she received other offers as well. The provision for that need had been laid up for her, but she could not access it with an unruly tongue, spewing words of unbelief.

The Hindrance to the Petition
(Unruly Tongue)

Although God *daily* loads us with benefits, [1] our goods are often under *siege*. They are held captive by a false tongue. Proverbs 6 explains how the siege works; it says: *"Thou are snared with the words of thy mouth; thy are taken with the words of thy mouth."* We miss it on this level when our tongue is unruly; [2] disobeying the law of faith.

The tongue sets the course of our lives. As the rudder, it sets us on the path of life or death; blessings or curses. With the tongue, we license either fallen angels to bring negative words to pass, or ministering spirits to bring positive words to pass. We are also *defiled* by the idle words that we speak, for words produce after their kind. And when we are double-tongued—making contrary declarations on the same subject—we cause a breach in the promises of God.

God had promised the children of Israel a land flowing with milk and honey. When Moses sent the twelve spies to search out the land in preparation for possessing it, ten of the twelve returned with an evil report. They acknowledged that the land was good and that it *was* flowing with milk and honey, but because there were giants in the land, they could not take it. They said that the people were stronger than they. To make matters worse, they saw *themselves* as grasshoppers.[3]

Because of the words of the ten spies, the children of Israel changed God's plan for their lives. They were not defeated by the giants—they were defeated by the power of the tongue *declaring* a grasshopper image.

The unruly member:

Although the tongue is a little member, it conducts itself in a disorderly fashion. Being unruly, it is evil and full of deadly poison. It can speak wisdom from below that is earthly, sensual, and devilish, and it also speaks wisdom from above that is peaceable, gentle, and easy to be entreated—full of mercy and good fruits— without hypocrisy.[4] When the tongue speaks wisdom from below, we find ourselves praying the way of the hypocrites—not receiving the reward of faith.

The Bible also says that the tongue is a fire, a world of iniquity that can only be kept at bay when the *flesh* is not fed. Proverbs 26:20 says: *"Where no wood is, there the fire goeth out."* Being a wood vessel, the flesh loves devouring words, whether they are directed at self or at others. It wants to destroy your right standing with God. And when the flesh is allowed to reign over the tongue, the whole body becomes defiled. The Bible says, *it is not that which goes into the mouth defiles a man; but that which comes out of the mouth, this defiles a man... those things which proceed out of the mouth come forth from the heart; and they defile the man.*[5]

It is the tongue, alone, that contaminates the heart; giving some a hard heart, others an offended heart, and still others a distracted heart. [6] All professing Jesus as Lord, but are fruitless. And often, when our natural provisions are held captive because of an unruly tongue, we blame God.

How often are we snared by our own tongue? [7] First, we encounter an obstacle and speak ill-advisedly over the situation. Then, when our negative words come to pass, we sit back and proudly say, "I knew it... just as I thought." In reality, using our tongue to speak evil, we have sabotaged the outcome. We bought into the fruit of the enemy. Until we order our conversation aright, we will not see the salvation of the Lord. Order, as defined by Webster's 1828 Dictionary, is ... *to be subject to rules or laws.* An unruly tongue does not obey the law of faith. And, without faith you cannot please God.

The Strategy to Escape the Hindrance
(Taming the Tongue)

Vessel of wood:

An unbridled tongue deceives our hearts. Paul, in 2 Timothy 2: 20-21, talks about a great house. In a great house there are vessels of gold and silver (symbolizing our spirit and soul). There are also vessels of wood and earth (symbolizing our flesh and body). There are some to honor, some to dishonour. Paul said that there are contaminating influences coming from our vessels of dishonor (wood and earth) disqualifying us from the Master's use. But if a man would purge himself of these, he would be a vessel of honor; meet for the Master's use.

The wood (representing our flesh) is the part of our being that must be addressed, *daily*. It must be crucified (put in order) daily. God calls it ordering our conversation aright. [8]

In 1 Kings 18, God had promised to send rain to end a drought that came as a result of the children of Israel halting between two opinions. They were not sure whether to serve God or Baal. Elijah proposed a contest to see who the real God was. To win this contest, Elijah would first have to deal with the wood-the area of contamination.

When it was his turn, the Bible says he *put the wood in order...* He poured water (representing the Word of God) on the burnt sacrifice and on the wood.[9] Elijah dealt with the wood. As a result, the children of Israel chose God and four hundred and fifty (450) false prophets of Baal were slayed. Afterwards, Elijah said that he heard the sound of rain. After praying and seeing a little cloud, there was a great rain. Putting the wood in order ended the drought.

Also, when God called Abraham, in Genesis 22, to offer his son upon the altar for a burnt offering, the Bible says: "*...and Abraham built an altar there, and laid the wood in order...*" [10] So Abraham also dealt with the wood, and Psalms 50:23 tells us that he who *orders* his conversation aright will see the salvation of God.

As Abraham stretched forth his hand to slay his son, the angel of the Lord called unto him and said, *"Abraham, lay not your hand upon the lad, neither do him no harm for I know that you fear God."* Next, Abraham lifted up his eyes and looked, and behind him was a ram caught in a thicket. So Abraham took the ram and offered it up for a burnt offering, instead of his son. Abraham called the name of that place Jehovah-Jireh, the Lord our Provider.

Abraham's physical provision (the ram) was tied to his spiritual obedience. In *ordering his conversation aright* he saw the salvation of the Lord. Abraham was able to receive his *daily* benefits from God, because he had not been taken captive by evil words. His words: *"God will provide a sacrifice of His own,"* brought peace to his heart and allowed virtue to flow as he controlled his tongue.

The Process of Effectual Prayer
Believing and Receiving

(Guarding the Promise)

This process focuses on <u>guarding</u> the promises of God by *only believing*; to avail much.

Mark 11:24

- Wisdom (what): *"Therefore I say unto you, what things so ever ye desire*
- Understanding (why): *when ye pray*
- Knowledge (how): *believe that ye receive them, and ye shall have them."*

The Bible said that Abraham staggered not at the promises of God through unbelief, but he was strong in the faith, giving glory to God; being fully persuaded that what God had promised He was able to perform. [11]

Abraham's father, on the other hand, settled. He never reached the land he had originally set out for. The Bible said he left to go into the land of Canaan, but he dwelt (settled) in Haran and died in Haran. [12] He failed to hold the beginning of his confidence steadfast to the end; therefore, he could not see the end of his faith, or the salvation of his soul.

Abraham did not *receive* wavering. The Bible said they went forth to go into the land of Canaan, and into the land of Canaan they came. [13] Additionally, being not weak in faith, he considered not his own body, nor the deadness of Sara's womb. His secret: He only considered the Word of God. Once you pray, the confession is: *I have already received it.* Therefore, you must aggressively fight wavering and refuse to settle for a lesser promise.

Keeping the enemy in the arena of faith:

While believing for a large amount of money, I was bombarded with thoughts of doubt. To which I responded by saying, "I have already received it." But the thoughts continued to come, disturbing my time of devotion. Nevertheless, I stood fast, speaking the same words: "But I have already received it." I was fully persuaded. Eventually, the thoughts stopped coming and a few days later, I received the full amount. To receive what has been given us by grace, the enemy must be kept in the arena of faith.

Give Us This Day Our Daily Bread

Key elements of this petition:

The Hindrance to this petition lies in a failure to receive, based on an unruly tongue. When we pray and fail to receive, it is not a prayer problem, it is a heart problem. God is not holding up our provisions, He's endeavoring to get them to us. Psalms 21:2 says: *"Thou has given him his heart's desire, has not withheld the request of his lips."* We are hindered from receiving either by being snared and taken captive by the words of our mouths, or because we fail to endure to the end.

The Strategy calls for us to pray, and *set a watch against the enemy of our soul day and night;* and, *bring into captivity every thought to the obedience of Christ.* (2 Corinthians 10:5)

Through the Process of Praying we must fight wavering; the Bible says everyone who asks receives. Although God answered Daniel's prayer the first day, he had to persist in prayer for twenty-one days before the answer could reach him. (Daniel 10:13)

Give us this day our daily bread, calls for us to communicate (speak) our faith; giving the Prayer of Petition the power to operate on behalf of our *daily* provisions; being empowered by Jehovah Jireh - the Lord our Provider.

The Prayer of Petition

This prayer involves petitioning God for our needs; it allows us to pray according to His will; His will is His Word. If we know that He hears us, then we have the petition we have desired of Him.[14]

- Wisdom (what): *"Be careful for nothing; but in everything by prayer and supplication with thanksgiving let your requests be made known unto God.*
- Understanding (why): *And the peace of God, which passeth all understanding, shall keep your hearts and minds through Christ Jesus.*
- Knowledge (how): *Finally, brethren, whatsoever things are true, whatsoever things are honest, whatsoever things are just, whatsoever things are pure, whatsoever things are lovely, whatsoever things are of good report; if there be any virtue, and if there be any praise, think on these things"* (Philippians 4:6-8).

This prayer is sometimes called the Prayer of Faith, where we make a petition to God. When we are in faith, we see things from God's perspective; we pray God's Word. According to Isaiah 55:11, God's word will not return void. It is for this reason that wicked Haman, in Esther 5:13, worried about Mordecai praying at the gate. None of his plots, plans, or wiles would profit him as long as prayer was consistently going forth: *"Yet all this availeth me nothing, so long as I see Mordecai the Jew sitting at the king's gate."*

When King Jehoshaphat and the children of Israel were under attack, he pleaded his case as he put forth a prayer of petition. And, God released a plan of attack that routed the enemy. The Bible recounts King Jehoshaphat's prayer of petition in 2 Chronicles 20:1-25:

Jehoshaphat *reminded* God of His Word:

Jehoshaphat, reminding God of His Word, prayed: "*If, when evil cometh upon us, as the sword, judgment, or pestilence, or famine, we stand before this house, and in thy presence, (for thy name is in this house,) and cry unto thee in our affliction, then thou wilt hear and help*" (2 Chronicles 20:9).

Jehoshaphat *petitioned* God:

"*And now, behold, the children of Ammon and Moab and mount Seir, whom thou wouldest not let Israel invade, when they came out of the land of Egypt, but they turned from them, and destroyed them not; Behold, I say, how they reward us, to come to cast us out of thy possession, which thou hast given us to inherit. O our God, wilt thou not judge them? For we have no might against this great company that cometh against us; neither know we what to do: but our eyes are upon thee*" (2 Chronicles 20:10-12).

God *answered* Jehoshaphat:

"*Ye shall not need to fight in this battle: set yourselves, stand ye still, and see the salvation of the* LORD *with you, O Judah and Jerusalem: fear not, nor be dismayed; tomorrow go out against them: for the* LORD *will be with you*" (2 Chronicles 20:17).

God gave them the *plan for victory*:

"*And they rose early in the morning, and went forth into the wilderness of Tekoa: and as they went forth, Jehoshaphat stood and said, Hear me, O Judah, and ye inhabitants of Jerusalem; Believe in the* LORD *your God, so shall ye be established; believe his prophets, so shall ye prosper. And when he had consulted with the people, he appointed singers unto the* LORD, *and that should praise the beauty of holiness, as they went out before the army, and to*

say, Praise the LORD; for his mercy endureth forever. And when they began to sing and to praise, the LORD set ambushments against the children of Ammon, Moab, and mount Seir, which were come against Judah; and they were smitten... and they were three days in gathering of the spoil, it was so much"
(2 Chronicles 20:20-25).

Petitioning God for *our* way of escape:

Although most of us think of a vision as a formal plan for our lives, it is also a day-to-day, moment-by-moment instruction or clarification, as well. Practically speaking, a vision may be a needed word, or a <u>counter-thought</u> against the attacks of the wicked. Jehoshaphat sought a *vision* from God and found that He longs to be gracious to us. God delights in empowering us to win every battle. When He is petitioned, he will always show us a way of escape.

Jehovah Jireh - the Lord our Provider

Genesis 22:14

God not only provides for us, but He also looks ahead and makes provision for us. God has a supply for all of our needs.[15] In the Bible, David declared that he *had never seen the righteous forsaken nor his seed begging bread.*[16] When we *do* find ourselves in need, we should check up on our confessions of faith.

Jehovah Jireh was there for the widow woman:

In 2 Kings 4, a certain woman came to the prophet Elisha and told him that her husband was dead *and that the creditor had come to take her two sons to be slaves.* Elisha asked her what was in her house. She said nothing, except a pot of oil. Elisha then gave her an instruction. She followed his instructions until the oil stayed and until there were no more empty vessels; by enduring till the end, she saw the end of her faith. He then told her to go sell the oil and pay thy debt with the proceeds, and then she and her children would have enough to live off of what was left. Jehovah Jireh provided for her: By believing His prophet, she operated in the Process of Effectual Prayer and she prospered.

Jehovah Jireh was there for the four lepers:

In 2 Kings 7, there was a famine in the land. Speaking the Word of God, the Prophet Elisha declared, basically, that tomorrow they will experience a due season. Meanwhile, there were four leprous men who sat at the gate. *They <u>said</u> to each other, why sit we here until we die?* They reasoned that they had nothing to lose by taking a risk and doing what was in their hearts. Walking by faith, they went into the enemy's camp. There, God used the sound of their steps of *faith* to rout the enemy. Instead of dying, they saved themselves and the city from a famine. Jehovah Jireh provided.

Jehovah Jireh
Promises Kept in His Name

❖ Because the Lord is our Provider, He shall: *"...supply all your need according to his riches in glory by Christ Jesus"* (Philippians 4:19).

❖ Because the Lord is our Provider, He shall daily load you with benefits, even the God of our salvation.(Psalms 68:19)

❖ Because the Lord is our Provider, *"...The barrel of meal shall not waste; neither shall the cruse of oil fail, until the day that the LORD sends rain upon the earth"* (1 Kings 17:14).

❖ Because the Lord is our Provider, in your prosperity you shall never be moved. (Psalms 30:6)

❖ Because the Lord is our Provider, *"I will abundantly bless her provision: I will satisfy her poor with bread"* (Psalms 132:15).

❖ Because the Lord is our Provider, God looks ahead and makes provision for us. (Genesis 22:14)

❖ Because the Lord is our Provider, *"The blessing of the Lord will make you rich, and add no sorrow with it"* (Proverbs 10:22).

Call to Action:

1. Ask the Lord to teach you to hold your tongue; to help you understand where you have erred. Declare a divine crop failure over <u>vain</u> words that you have spoken; then loose a bumper crop over words you have spoken that are <u>in line with His Will</u>. Purpose to keep your mouth with a bridle while the wicked is before you.

2. *"The night is far spent, the day is at hand: let us therefore cast off the works of darkness, and let us put on the armour of light"* (Romans 13:12).

3. Now, release the supply for your need. Command it to come to you, saying: "Go ministering spirits; cause my supply to come to me... I believe I receive it in Jesus' Name, Amen."

Pray:
I said, I will take heed to my ways, that I sin not with my tongue: I will keep my mouth with a bridle, while the wicked is before me. (Psalms 39:1)

Confess:
In my tongue is the law of kindness.

Chapter 4

1. Psalms 68:19
2. James 3:8
3. Numbers 13:33
4. James 3:15-17
5. Matthew 15:11-20
6. Matthew 13
7. Proverbs 6:2
8. Psalms 50:23
9. 1 Kings 18:33
10. Genesis 22:9
11. Romans 4:20-21
12. Genesis 11:31-32
13. Genesis 12:1-5
14. 1 John 5:15
15. Philippians 4:19
16. Psalms 37:25

And forgive us our debts,
as we forgive our debtors.

Chapter 5

Deliverance through the Love Walk

*A*nd forgive us our debts, as we forgive our debtors, evokes the Prayer of Confession—the need for a clean conscience. Through this prayer we call on Jehovah Rapha - the Lord our Healer, to heal the broken-hearted. The strategy for this petition addresses the need to walk in love. Operating the Process of Dominion, we start with binding the attacks against our peace.

A few years ago, I was faced with an issue where I wanted a certain person to *'reap what was sown.'* I was evoking the old wives' tale: *You made your bed hard, now you must lie in it.* Others agreed with me, but God let me know that although *the way of the transgressor is hard*, we still have to walk the love walk; especially, the 'royal law'—where you love your neighbor as yourself. This law, in effect, says: It's not that you didn't do anything wrong, I'm just not holding it against you.

The next day, I awoke from a dream with the overwhelming feeling that I had really pleased God. He was literally, happy with me. The dream showed me walking in the 'royal law,' handling the situation by faith. That day, I found myself going above and beyond the call of duty on behalf of that individual.

The Hindrance to the Petition
(Unclean Heart)

When we miss it on this level, we are operating as an *accuser of the brethren*.[1] We owe each other love, but we have turned from our righteous nature, and are now making decisions based on the hearing of our ears and judging after the sight of the eyes, yet this judgment does *not* minister to their hearts. Without love, we only see in part—we cannot pay the debt of love that we owe.

In Matthew 18, the story is told of a man who owed ten thousand talents to his lord. Because he did not have it to pay, he and all of his family were to be sold. The man begged for patience, and it was given to him. He was, no doubt, relieved that his trespasses were not held against him.

Later, this same man (who had *received* patience) was in a position to *grant* patience to his fellowman. The Bible says he went out and found one of his fellowservants who owed him just an hundred pence. He grabbed him and demanded that he pay what was owed. Seeing that he did not have it to pay, the fellowservant also begged for patience, but he was not given it; he was then cast into prison until he should pay the debt. Others who witnessed the event went and reported it, and when confronted by his lord as to why he did not give the patience that the situation required, the man was speechless. Afterwards, he and his family were turned over to the tormentors until the love was paid.

Jesus said that this is what happens when we fail to forgive— when we do not love others as God has loved us. We accuse others and excuse *ourselves*. When we do unto others as we would have them do unto us, only then is the mind guarded against the torment of unforgiveness.

The Strategy to Escape the Hindrance
(Love Walk)

"Again, the kingdom of heaven is like unto treasure hid in a field; the which when a man hath found, he hideth, and for joy thereof goeth and selleth all that he hath, and buyeth that field." [2]

Loving the Unlovely

Although the thoughts of the righteous are right, the unlovely *buy into* those thoughts that that appeal to our weaker nature: our field. The enemy works the field by stealing our peace—the guardian of the soul. He renders it unlovely. Fortunately, the field is offset by treasure and through walking the love walk, we find the treasure.

So, there is a treasure hidden inside each of us, but we also have a field. We have a spirit and we have a flesh. We have a sin nature, but we also have Christ in us, the hope of glory.[3] We travel from one part of our being to the other part by our thoughts. We are either *turning* to buy into thoughts from the treasure or we are *turning* to buy into thoughts from the field. And, if the field is not fortified with the fruit of the Spirit, the *field* becomes a dangerous place to be in:

- Cain killed Able in the field.
- Esau was faint in the field when he sold his birthright.
- The elder brother of the prodigal son was angry in the field.
- Joseph was wandering in the field before his brothers threw him in the pit.
- We waste away for lack of the fruits of the field.

The field, indeed, represents a dilemma for us. It renders us as double-agents; when we want to do good, evil is present.[4] Nevertheless, we <u>do</u> have this treasure in our earthen vessels. Yet, in order to get to the treasure, we must 'sell' all: doubt, unbelief, care, and fear; then, through faith spoken words, 'buy' that field. If *we* don't buy that field, the enemy will.

In the book of Ruth, the enemy (a type of flesh) was able to buy (overcome) Naomi's land, because she was in bitterness of soul. Since bitterness is from the kingdom of darkness, he had a right to her land and the treasure it contained. 5

But Ruth was a different story; she was walking in the fruit of the Spirit—love, not fulfilling the lust of her flesh. The enemy could not buy her field—she had sold all that *belonged* to the kingdom of darkness.

Don't give up on others:

In Jeremiah 32:7-27, God told Jeremiah, *"Go buy the field."* Jeremiah was perplexed: Why would anyone want to buy such a worthless field; especially since we are about to go into captivity? God basically explained to him that he was planning a turnaround: that houses, fields, and vineyards shall again be possessed in this land... Finally God said, *"Behold, I am the Lord, God of all flesh: Is there anything too hard for me?"*

As in all drama, the flesh is first on the scene; it has first dibs. But, the Lord has the final Word. God knows how to deliver the godly out of temptations and reserve the unjust unto the day of judgment to be punished. (2 Peter 2:9) Getting flesh up to par is nothing for God. In Romans 14:4, God said, He can make us all stand. God asserts, *"Who are you to judge another man's servant. To His own Master he will stand or fall. And stand he will, for I am able to make him stand."*

Furthermore, God says those whom we despise, thinking that they are worthless dirt (fields), are in fact rich in faith and heirs of the kingdom. 6 (There is *treasure* in their fields.)

God knows that unless *you* buy the field to get the treasure, the righteous would be destroyed with the wicked, God forbid.

And throughout the Bible, God has asked us *not to throw the baby away with the bath water.*

God says:

- Don't throw away Joseph; you will need him to protect you against the famine.
- Don't throw away the prodigal son; one day he will come to himself and say, *"I will return to my father's house."*
- Don't throw away Peter; once he is converted, he will strengthen the brethren.
- Don't give up on Saul; he will become Paul and preach the faith that he once destroyed.
- Don't give up on Job; Job himself said, *"... when he has tried me, I shall come forth as gold."*
- And Joseph, don't put away Mary; she shall bring forth a Son and call His name Jesus, and He shall save His people from their sins.

Without the fruit of the Spirit, we would all lean to our own understanding and trust in our own hearts; then throw away the good with the bad. We owe each other love. And the debt of love is paid through patience.

Moody, a Joint that Supplieth

Forgive us our debts, as we forgive our debtors involves loving others unconditionally. During a Bible study, I asked a question about the love covenant. My brother-in-law, Dr. Moody Jackson, answered the question with one of the most profound insights I had ever heard. He explained so eloquently that because of the New Covenant, we have been given a new commandment. We are no longer required to love our neighbor as ourselves. Now, we are required to love one another as God has loved us. Furthermore, this new commandment is also unconditional—remarkably, it requires only one person to keep it.

God has raised the bar! I cannot tell you the number of persons who have been set free with this wisdom alone. Before this revelation, I spent hours trying to convince others why they should forgive. Dr. Jackson's wisdom cut to the chase and as the book of Hebrews says: *"Stops the mouths of lions."* It ends all arguments.

Moody, indeed, is a joint that supplieth. Ephesians 4 says every joint supplieth. 7 As a *body* of believers, we supply vital nutrients to one another—supplying the knowledge that is needed for our deliverance. To cut off a joint is to cut off a supply with its treasure.

Keeping Each Joint Supplying

To keep each joint supplying, begins with keeping our hearts cleansed by confessing our sins, for He is faithful and just to forgive us our sins and cleanse us from all unrighteousness. (1 John 1:9) A young lady was caught up in an indiscretion involving medication, and God was dealing with her on the issue. She confessed her error to a group of us and shared that she was uncomfortable continuing in that direction. I received a vison that as soon as she confessed it, darkness left her heart. She was not only forgiven, but she was cleansed, as well.

Prayer and forgiveness:

To keep each joint suppling, we are to be kind to one another, tenderhearted, and forgiving—even as God, for Christ's sake, has forgiven us. (Ephesians 4:32)

Mark 11:25-26, connects <u>forgiveness to prayer</u>: *"And when ye stand praying, forgive, if ye have ought against any: that your Father also which is in heaven may forgive you your trespasses. But if ye do not forgive, neither will your Father which is in heaven forgive your trespasses."*

Forgiveness and forgetting:

Isaiah 43:25 connects <u>forgiveness to forgetting:</u> God says, "*I, even I, am he that blotted out thy transgressions for mine own sake, and <u>will not remember thy sins</u>.*" Here, God is saying I have to forgive you, because I need you. There is an assignment that only clean hearts can accomplish. Lives are at stake.

We, too, must forgive and not remember the sin, for our own sake, as well. Unforgiveness cuts us off physically as well as spiritually. It also releases the tormentors—you will have no peace of mind.

Maturity and forgetting:

The *mature,* according to Paul, forget those things that are behind and press toward the mark for the prize of the high calling of God in Christ Jesus. (Philippian 3:13-14)

Violating the Love Law

Love endures long and is patient and kind; it takes no account of evil done to it; love pays no attention to a suffered wrong. [8] Love is adaptable.

When my nephew, Frederick, was an adolescent, he was often praised for his a great memory. One day, I overheard him talking about how he had been mistreated. He had remembered each incident: when he was five, this person did this to him at school, and how his cousin did this and that when he was six...and so on.

Alarmed, I took him to the side and said, "That's the wrong use of your memory. You are violating the Love Law; love takes no account of evil done to it; it pays no attention to a suffered wrong. You are acting like a prosecutor: count one, count two...etc. But love covers all sins." [9] We then went over the Love Law in 1 Corinthians 13 (Amplified Version). He got the picture immediately; saw where he had missed it. He judged himself and adjusted his heart.

Walking the Love Walk

I was led to give a few remarks at the home going of a close relative. Prior to my remarks I had a vision of the number *zero*, and the Holy Spirit gave me a word of knowledge relative to this individual. It expressed that he had left this world owing no man nothing—he had paid everyone the love that he owed.

As relatives and others spoke of him, all I heard was love. Even though some of the topics they had discussed with him were controversial and would have raised the brow of some, his responses yielded no condemnation. This manner of communication validated them as individuals. Their hearts were safe with him. And although he was a regular guy, when he passed, there were at least three memorial services held to honor him.

This man had faced the same tests and trails of life as others, but he kept the first things first—as individuals crossed his path he paid them the love he owed them. Walking in the identity of his anointing, he fulfilled the *'royal law':* loving thy neighbor as thyself.[10] By the way, his parents named him, *Royal.* Now from the other side of the grave, he still epitomized the sentiments, "I paid you the love I owed you." That's a legacy!

The Process of Dominion
Binding and Loosing

(Guarding Your Heart and Mind)

This process focuses on allowing the peace of God to rule our hearts and minds—as an unguarded heart is unpredictable.

Hebrews 12:14-15
- Wisdom (what): *"Follow peace with all men, and holiness,*
- Understanding (why): *without which no man shall see the Lord*
- Knowledge (how): *Looking diligently lest any man fail of the grace of God; lest any root of bitterness springing up trouble you, and thereby many be defiled."*

The tests of life are independent of the circumstances, and we are only called to pass the test. This is done by guarding the heart, for out of it flows the issues of life.[11] Consider Ruth, Naomi, and Orpah: three women, all of whom faced the same storm. Each one's husband died, and all became poverty stricken. Yet, each dealt with it differently: Orpah backslid, Naomi became bitter, but Ruth received a better resurrection.[12] She married into wealth and became part of the lineage of King David. If Ruth had yielded to bitterness, she would not have received her supply. By guarding her heart, she allowed the issue of peace to flow. By passing the test, she changed her circumstances.

When peace flows, it empowers us to walk in our dominion. By guarding our hearts and minds, we bind and loose forces of darkness. Matthew 18 says: whatsoever we *bind* on earth shall be *bound* in heaven. And whatsoever we *loose* on earth shall be *loosed* in heaven. The Name of Jesus gives us the power of attorney to bind and loose. It is in this Name that every knee shall bow in heaven and in earth; we forbid things that are deemed unlawful (under the new covenant) from coming into our lives. Basically, we don't receive them. And we loose those things, deemed by heaven, that are lawful. Those lacking peace are loosed from torment. In His name we also have commanding power. We can command forces of darkness to cease and desist in their maneuvers against us, and loose them from their assignment against us, in Jesus' name.

The purpose of binding and loosing is to <u>maintain our peace</u> within ourselves and with men. We forbid the forces of darkness from coming against us through flesh and blood.

We have but one enemy, and it is not man. The Bible calls him the *accuser of the brethren*. He defiles through works of the flesh. When the heart is not guarded, he contaminates it through strife, bitterness and unforgiveness. And unforgiveness releases all the forces of darkness against us; it gives them free reign.

And although we are owed love, we employ the fruit of patience until the debt is paid. Being moved with *compassion*, we are empowered to loose the transgressor and forgive the debt (of love owed to us), lest any root of bitterness springing up trouble us and defile the body.[13] God calls <u>forgiveness, checkmate</u>!

Forgive Us Our Debts, As We Forgive Our Debtors

Key elements of this petition:

The Hindrance to this petition lies in keeping account of evil done to us, or paying attention to a suffered wrong: unforgiveness.

The Strategy calls for us to love one another as God has loved us: unconditionally. This kind of love is not performance based: it can't be increased or decreased. It is merciful. It bears up under anything and everything that comes. And it never fails.

Through the Process of Dominion, we let the peace of God guard our hearts and minds. An unguarded heart is unpredictable.

Forgive us our debts, as we forgive our debtors, allows mercy to triumph over judgment; giving the Prayer of Confession the power to forgive us and cleanse us from all unrighteousness; being empowered by Jehovah Rapha – the Lord our Healer.

The Prayer of Confession
(Judging Thyself)

1 John 1:7-9

- Wisdom (what): *"But if we walk in the light, as he is in the light, we have fellowship one with another and the blood of Jesus Christ his Son cleanseth us from all sin.*
- Understanding (why): *If we say that we have no sin, we deceive ourselves, and the truth is not in us.*
- Knowledge (how): *If we confess our sins, he is faithful and just to forgive us our sins, and to cleanse us from all unrighteousness."*

Although we have been forgiven of our sins, and God is not holding anything against us, from time to time we still need to be cleansed from things that violate our conscience, such as errors of commission (things we did wrong) and omission (things we failed to do).[14] These are things that give place to the enemy.[15] David confessed his sins and asked for forgiveness following his infidelity with Bathsheba:

"Have mercy upon me, O God, according to thy lovingkindness: according unto the multitude of thy tender mercies blot out my transgressions.

Wash me thoroughly from mine iniquity, and cleanse me from my sin.

For I acknowledge my transgressions: and my sin is ever before me.

Against thee, thee only, have I sinned, and done this evil in thy sight: that thou mightest be justified when thou speakest, and be clear when thou judgest.

Behold, I was shaped in iniquity; and in sin did my mother conceive me. Behold, thou desires truth in the inward parts: and in the hidden part thou shalt make me to know wisdom.

Purge me with hyssop, and I shall be clean: wash me, and I shall be whiter than snow.

Make me to hear joy and gladness; that the bones which thou hast broken may rejoice.

Hide thy face from my sins, and blot out all mine iniquities.

<u>*Create in me a clean heart*</u>, *O God; and renew a right spirit within me.*

Cast me not away from thy presence; and take not thy holy spirit from me.

Restore unto me the joy of thy salvation; and uphold me with thy free spirit" (Psalms 51:1-12).

David behaved himself wisely, following his indiscretion, to avoid condemnation:

- First he confessed his faults (that he may be healed).
- Next he judged himself (so that he will not be judged).
- Then he forgave himself (as he would forgive others).
- And, he moved on (free of condemnation).

Forgive them for searching for love:

The hungry soul is searching for fruit. Their cry is: let me come into your garden and eat your pleasant fruit. [16]

At the end of a full day, I found myself becoming irritated by the taunt of a nephew. I wanted to give him a piece of my mind, or at the least, put him in his place. As I was about to *turn* myself to address him, the Holy Spirit stopped me and said, "He's searching for love." This wisdom changed my perception. I was then able to respond in a more gentle fashion, and the relationship was spared the disruption.

The flesh manipulates our perceptions to bring its purposes to pass. Its purpose is to keep us in the natural, to stop the anointing. But when the natural is all you see, the natural is all you will ever have. Forgiveness however, keeps us in the anointing.

When Jesus said, *"Father, forgive them; for they know not what they do,"* [17] He knew that the crowd was searching for love. They had seen how He handled the hypocrites: *"You whited-walled sepultures."* And how He handled evil: *"Get thee behind me, Satan."* But how would He handle those who returned Him evil for His good? Jesus' response released a love that changed the world forever.

On the cross, Jesus passed the 'love the unlovely' test: *"...for he is kind unto the unthankful and to the evil."* [18] Like Jesus, our response to the unlovely should be: *Come into my garden and eat my pleasant fruit.*

Tarry for them:

From time to time, we find ourselves in situations where others are not up to par—they are lying down on the job. The snare is for us to point the finger (judging another man's servant), or touching God's anointed. Usually, I guard my heart and hold my peace, but on one occasion, I did not. The Holy Spirit stopped me, warning that I should not go there, lest I come into condemnation. He cited 1 Corinthians 11:33-34 and admonished me to tarry for the individual—give them time to turn around—pray for them that their faith would not fail. Intentionally overcoming evil with good, I began to bless and not curse. A couple of years later, God brought the person back up to par. Now that person is better than ever. God made the person *stand.*

Jehovah Rapha – the Lord our Healer

Exodus 15:26

The Lord Jehovah Rapha is there to heal the broken hearted. He is there helping us not to sorrow as those without hope. He is the Lord our Healer; even healing the wounded spirit and the bitterness of soul.

Jehovah Rapha was there for Hannah:

In 1 Samuel 1, the story is told about a woman named Hannah who was in bitterness of soul, because she had no children. The Bible said her adversary provoked her sore, to make her fret, because the Lord had shut up her womb. Hannah also described *herself* as being a woman of a sorrowful spirit; however, she refused to give up on her dream. In the house of the Lord, Hannah poured out her soul before the Lord. Eventually, the man of God, Eli, gave her a word of knowledge and said: Go on peace and God would grant thee thy petition. And the Lord remembered her. She conceived, bared a son, and called his name Samuel.

Hannah worked her covenant and discovered that Jehovah Rapha was there for her. By going in peace, Hannah guarded her heart and mind. With this act, she operated in the Process of Dominion.

Jehovah Rapha
Promises Kept in His Name

❖ Because the Lord is your Healer: *"He healeth the broken in heart, and bindeth up their wounds"* (Psalms 147:3).

❖ Because the Lord is your Healer: *"...for he satisfieth the longing soul, and filleth the hungry soul with goodness"* (Psalms 107:9).

❖ Because the Lord is your Healer: *"The LORD is nigh unto them that are of a broken heart; and saveth such as be of a contrite spirit"* (Psalms 34:18).

❖ Because the Lord is your Healer: *"For thus saith the high and lofty One that inhabits eternity, whose name is Holy; I dwell in the high and holy place, with him also that is of a contrite and humble spirit, to revive the spirit of the humble, and to revive the heart of the contrite ones"* (Isaiah 57:15).

❖ Because the Lord is your Healer: *"... to this man will I look, even to him that is poor and of a contrite spirit, and trembleth at my word"* (Isaiah 66:2).

Call to Action:

1. Ask the Father to give you wisdom, understanding, and largeness of heart. Ask Him to help you to regard no man after the flesh, see the poor as rich in faith and heirs of salvation, and not destroy the righteous with the wicked.

2. *"Put on therefore, as the elect of God, holy and beloved, bowels of mercies, kindness, humbleness of mind, meekness, longsuffering; forbearing one another, and forgiving one another, if any man have a quarrel against any: even as Christ forgave you, so also do ye. And above all these things put on charity, which is the bond of perfectness"* (Colossians 3:12-14).

3. Ask God to forgive them, for they know not what they do. Loose the blood to reconcile your relationship(s). Ask the Father to give you His peace to rule in your heart and mind.

Pray:
Father, I choose to forgive as an act of my free will. I loose the blood of Jesus to reconcile our relationship and bring about a healing of hearts. I judge myself so I will not be judged, in Jesus Name, Amen.

Confess:
...I sorrow not as those without hope. (1 Thessalonians 4:13)

Chapter 5

1. Revelation 12:10
2. Matthew 13:44
3. Colossians 1:27
4. Romans 7:21
5. Ruth 4
6. James 2:4-5
7. Ephesians 4:16
8. 1 Corinthians 13
9. Proverbs 10:12
10. James 2:8
11. Proverbs 4:23-27
12. Ruth 1; 4:13-17
13. Hebrews 12:15
14. 1 John 3:20
15. Ephesians 4:27
16. Song of Songs 4:16
17. Luke 23:34
18. Luke 6:35

And lead us not into temptation,
but deliver us from evil:

Chapter 6

Deliverance through Fighting the Inner Giant

*A*nd lead us not into temptation, but deliver us from evil, evokes the Prayer of Imprecation—the need to crucify the flesh. Through this prayer we call on Jehovah Nissi – the Lord our Banner, to bring vengeance upon the 'inner giant.' The strategy for this petition addresses the wicked counselor. Operating the Process of Avoiding Temptation, we start with praying the Lord's Prayer.

While at church, I was prompted to pray the Lord's Prayer. For some reason, I usually do so with another person—in a 'prayer of agreement' style. Shortly afterwards, my family made the decision to change seats (to move up closer to the pulpit).

So, we   gathered our belongings and made the move. As we settled in, the Holy Spirit reminded me that I had left my purse behind. The church was filling up, so I rushed back to our original seats, and thank God, it was still there. Through this petition, we are delivered from the evil plans of the wicked.

The Hindrance to the Petition
(Flesh: Inner Giant)

We miss it in this level when we give ear to what the Bible calls the *wicked counsellor*. Nahum 1:11 says: *"There is one come out of thee, that imagineth evil against the Lord, a wicked counselor."* It comes in the midst of us to frustrate our purposes. Through *perception, it* affects the: will, mind, emotions, intellect, and imaginations. It is this *giant* that influenced King David's involvement with Bathsheba.

In 2 Samuel 11, the Bible says that at the time when kings go forth to battle, King David sent his captain, Joab, and his servants to the battlefield; however, he tarried still at Jerusalem. But this decision lacked discernment, as it *was* a time of war. In reality, King David was fighting an inner war, and having lost that inner battle, he was out of agreement with God and subject to the carnal man. He couldn't walk in his authority, because he was walking in unbelief.

Despising the commandment of the Lord, King David had *turned* himself. He had failed to guard his heart. On the battlefield, his men did not have the benefit of his wisdom, and errors were made that needlessly cost lives. King David was also guilty of adultery and murder. One man's fall into temptation, impacted the lives of so many.

How did such a man, after God's own heart, end up in defeat? The answer can be found in Nehemiah 4:11: *"And our adversaries said, they shall not know, neither see, till we come in the midst among them, and slay them and cause the work to cease."* Basically, David never knew what hit him. He did not realize that he was being drawn away by his own desires and enticed. This wicked counselor that comes out of us may be *called* the 'inner giant,' but it is *named* the flesh. Simply put, this giant is the culprit behind every yield to temptation.

The Strategy to Escape the Hindrance
(Fruit of the Spirit)

"You have one more enemy to fight," said the Holy Spirit as I was awakening from a dream. In that dream, I had destroyed enemy, after enemy, after enemy—they had been mountains, but now they were plains. I was feeling good, until I finally reached the last enemy. I didn't know what hit me; it was man handling me. I wondered *what type of enemy was this?* It was the flesh, known as self, the perpetrator of the original sin.

Self wages a subtle and almost imperceptible battle for the control of our souls. It causes us to second guess all of our good efforts, preys on our emotions, fights against our anointing, and hinders our faith. Yet, it is largely *un-opposed.*

Self alienates us from the promises of God, defies our Christian walk, and makes a mockery out of our faith-walk. It is this enemy who *leads us into the temptation.*

Self also feeds on our natural senses. We call it perception (the way we view reality), but when our views of life violates the wisdom of God, He calls it *flesh.* The flesh manipulates our perceptions to bring its purposes to pass, and its primary purpose is to stop the anointing. The game plan of the flesh is to keep us in the natural realm (the area of its dominion), and if the natural is all we see, then the natural is all we will ever have.

"You are not your flesh," were the words the Holy Spirit gave me to tell my daughter. Not long afterwards, as she walked up the stairs, coming from her time of devotion, she said to me, "I just found out that it was not me doing all those silly things, it was my flesh."

The flesh is an *undercover* agent working on behalf of the enemy. Although it is not the body, it exerts pressure on the body. It is akin to scales on a fish. It is a kind of animal nature. It works to draw us away, using our own *strong* desires, to prepare us for the temptation.

Flesh manifests as a way of thinking that opposes the will of God. It fights against the spirit and the spirit fights against it.[1] The Bible says they are contrary one against the other. It usurps the will of God through the lure of *pleasant knowledge* (thoughts that seem right but they end in destruction). [2]

Consider Eve. She was tempted by pleasant knowledge (her own desire) and enticed. The Bible said that she saw that the tree was good for food, <u>pleasant</u> to the eyes, and to be desired to make one wise. However, by having no input from her spirit, she was not prepared to fight pleasant knowledge. Like Eve, we too, are not designed to fight the flesh, alone. We need the Helper. When she bought into the *perception* of the flesh, it kept her in the natural realm. This natural view alienates us from our anointing.

Faulty perceptions:

King Saul could not partake of the gifts and anointing of David because he saw him, in the natural, as a threat. [3] But those who *did* receive David's anointing were turned into mighty men.[4]

Gideon, seeing himself in the natural said, *"I am the least in my father's house."* [5] That perception kept him living under a spirit of poverty. Nevertheless, God changed his perception and that changed his reality. For when he saw himself the way God saw him (as a mighty man of valor), he was able to deliver the children of Israel from the Midianites.

A faulty perception can also cause us to make inaccurate assumptions: Paul's jailer, assuming that Paul and Silas had escaped from prison, almost killed himself. [6] And Abner, the captain of Saul's host, assumed that Joab (David's general) was there (in Hebron) to befriend him, not knowing that he was actually there to take his life. David said later, *"Died Abner as a fool dieth?"* [7]

Flesh battles:

The battle with the flesh is one of the greatest you will ever have to fight—it is a type of civil war battle where you must vehemently oppose *your 'self.'*

David, prior to taking the kingdom, was able to kill the outer giant, Goliath; even a lion and a bear.[8] But he was defeated by the giant within—the flesh slayed him with *guile.*

After the flood, Noah was naked, the flesh slayed him with thirst. In fact, Proverbs 1 warns that when we turn away from wisdom, [9] we will all be slayed by the flesh. The flesh limits our ability to release the supernatural powers resident within each of us. We become conformed to the image of the natural man.

In Genesis 49, Jacob, in blessing his twelve sons, began with his eldest: Rueben. He called him, *"...my might, and the beginning of my strength, the excellency of dignity, and the excellency of power."* [10] That says to me that when Rueben was born, Jacob was a proud father. But Jacob was never able to nurture the supernatural gift that he saw in Rueben. Rueben simply never bought into the blessing. Instead, he bought into the natural image of himself and the natural image was all he ever had. On Jacob's death bed, he called Rueben, *"Unstable as water."* [11]

Each son received a blessing from Jacob that showed the Father's heart toward them. Of the ten sons, only Joseph fought to maintain the image his father bestowed upon him. The flesh did everything to steal his image, for he was: stripped of his coat, thrown into a pit, sold as a slave, lied on, and put into prison. Yet Joseph resisted—he fought the image of the natural man, never internalizing the actions levied against him. He did not allow his flesh to reproach (belittle) him.

Joseph saw the end of his faith at the age of 30. He had fought till due season, and he finally became worthy of the favor bestowed on him by his father and by God. For thirteen years Joseph fought circumstances, experiences, and illusions from the flesh to become what God had ordained before the foundation of the world.

Joseph's main fear was: not possessing the promise God had for his life. In the book of Hebrews, God says we should all have this fear. [12] The children of Israel fell short of the promise God had for them; it was stolen by unbelief. We should all fear leaving a promise for our lives on the table. For when we fight the perception of the flesh, we possess the promise, and enter into His rest.

Fruitful bough:

In blessing Joseph, his father, Jacob, called him a fruitful bough—he bore good fruit. [13] And Joseph glorified our heavenly Father by bearing much fruit.

Some readers may have had parents who failed to bestow the blessing on them. No problem. The Jabez Prayer, found in 1 Chronicles 4:9-10, is for you. Jabez went directly to God. And the Bible says God granted him his request.

The Jabez Prayer

"And Jabez was more honourable than his brethren:
and his mother called his name Jabez, saying, Because I bare him
with sorrow [in the natural].

> *And Jabez called on the God of Israel,*
> *saying, Oh that thou wouldest bless me indeed,*
> *and enlarge my coast,*
> *and that thine hand might be with me,*
> *and that thou wouldest keep me from evil, that it may not*
> *grieve me!*
> *And God granted him that which he requested"*

(1 Chronicles 4:9-10).

Prepared for battle—the secret:

In John 15:8, the Bible says, *"Herein is my Father glorified,
that ye bear much fruit; so shall ye be my disciples."*

The production of fruit is what prepares us for the fiery darts
of the wicked. In warning Cain before his attack on Abel, God told
him that sin (nature) lies at the door and desires to have him, but he
must rule over him. But Cain failed to heed God's warning, and he
killed his brother. Now the ground of his heart shall not yield her
strength—it will be difficult to produce fruit; he will not be dressed
for battle.

On the other hand, Samson *was* prepared for battle. [14] Being
a Nazarite, he was unpruned. His fruit was always in place. As a fruit
bearing vine, he destroyed the enemy at every turn. When the
Philistines sought to exploit the secret of Samson's strength (how he
could become weak as any other man), they hired Delilah (a type of
flesh) to do it. Her job was to entice him. To do so, she would have to
get him into the flesh. So, using *his* own desires, she tempted him.
Samson eventually told her all his heart: things that he was in care

about—now he would be able to be enticed. She then called for a man to *shave* him; then she began to afflict him. In so doing, his strength went from him—she stopped his production of fruit. He became barren; as weak as any other man. Through the flesh, Delilah got him into the natural, and when the natural is all you see, the natural is all you will ever have. The natural puts us under the dominion of unbelief.

Jesus also experienced the limiting effect of the natural (unbelief) on His own ministry. When the Jews in His home town saw Him only as a carpenter's son, rather than as the Messiah, the Bible says there, He could do no mighty works. Neither could Samson. He became weak as another man and was put in prison—the house of the flesh: a vessel of destruction, fitted for wrath.

While being unpruned, Samson's focus was only against the evil intents of the enemy, not people. When his father-in-law gave his wife to his companion, being unpruned, Samson took no account of the evil they committed against him; he paid no attention to the suffered wrong. Instead, he took vengeance against the Philistines. When his own countrymen turned him over to the Philistines, being unpruned, he took no account of the evil they committed against him; he paid no attention to the suffered wrong. Again, he took vengeance against the Philistines.

Time after time, Samson came against the enemy of his soul, only. Our battle, the Bible says, is not against flesh and blood, it is against flesh only. And the flesh can only be defeated by the fruit of the Spirit.

The secret of Samson's strength was fruit bearing. As kryptonite is to Superman, the fruit of the Spirit is to the flesh. It is the only weapon against the flesh; its affections and lusts (strong desires). When we bear the fruit of the Spirit, we are prepared to crucify the inner giant.

In a race run all, the Bible says, but only one receives the prize: [15] you or your flesh. This race is a type of wager: the flesh is betting that you will not overcome him, and *you* have placed your bet on Christ in you, the hope of Glory. Pressing toward the mark, the race is on.

According to Romans 8:5, the key is the focus of the mind: *"For they that are after the flesh do mind the things of the flesh; but they that are after the Spirit the things of the Spirit. For to be carnally minded is death; but to spiritually minded is life and peace."*

The good news is that we are not in the flesh, but we are in the Spirit, if it be so that the Spirit of God dwells in us. [16] And when we are led of the Spirit, we are not under the law, [17] but we are free from the works of the flesh.

If we live in the Spirit, let us also walk in the Spirit.[18] God is saying don't live as hypocrites, live according to our new nature—the influence of the Spirit; the fruit of the Spirit: love, joy, peace, longsuffering, gentleness, goodness, faith, meekness, and temperance: against such there is no law.

Samson is a member of the Hebrews' Hall of Faith. [19] Like him, our wrath should only be reserved for the enemy of our souls. We are called to forsake vain glory, provoking one another, and envying. [20] The fruit of the Spirit keeps us prepared for the real battle: crucifying the flesh. The secret: being unpruned.

The Process of Avoiding Temptation
Watching and Praying

(Guarding Your Fruit)

This process focuses on being sober and vigilant; guarding attacks against the fruit of the Spirit—our issues of life.

Matthew 26:41
- Wisdom (what): *"Watch and pray,*
- Understanding (why): *that you enter not into temptation:*
- Knowledge (how): *the spirit indeed is willing, but the flesh is weak."*

When the enemy conspired, all of them together, to come and fight against Jerusalem and to hinder it, Nehemiah and the children of Israel made their prayer unto God, and they set a watch against them day and night. [21] They watched (became sober and vigilance) against thinking thoughts that were not in line with the will of God, against speaking words that were not in line with the will of God, and against receiving images that exalted themselves above the will of God. You could say, they thought on things that were: *true, honest, just, pure, lovely, and of a good report*—only thoughts that produced virtue and praise.[22]

And, *unlike Samson*, when he was pressured by Delilah to reveal his care, Nehemiah said he gave the enemy of his soul the same answer each time. He never wavered. *"And I sent messengers unto them, saying, I am doing a great work, so that I cannot come <u>down</u>: why should the work cease, whilst I leave it, and come <u>down</u> to you? Yet they sent unto me <u>four times</u> after this sort; and I answered them after the same manner"* (Nehemiah 6:3-4). One lady said she had to fight the same thought for eight times, before it left her. She had to be steadfast. She won the battle against her soul.

Nehemiah was able to win battle after battle against the opposition, because he had won the battle within. One pastor said it this way, *"It does not matter who the opposition is. When you can win the battle within, you can win the battle without."* Nevertheless, when the enemy is within, the Helper is needed. It is a job for the Holy Spirit, and it is time to pray the Lord's Prayer. God then reveals the enemy's plans, bringing his counsel to nought.

And Lead Us Not Into the Temptation, but Deliver Us From Evil

Key elements of this petition:

The Hindrance to this petition lies in failing to watch and pray. We begin in the spirit, then turn to obey thoughts from the flesh. One moment Peter, responding to his spirit, declared Jesus as the Christ, the next, he responded to his flesh: echoing sentiments to prevent Jesus from fulfilling the will of God.

Although the flesh is our weakest link, it does not play fair. It endeavors to catch us when we are off guard. Coming in the midst of us, it searches for fears, cares, pleasant knowledge, and even strong desires, to ensnare us. Psalms 37:32-33 says: *"The wicked watcheth the righteous, and seeketh to slay him."* But the Lord's Prayer takes us from one step of faith to the next, to build our wall of defense, causing us to win the inner battle.

The Strategy calls for us to be focused, sober, and vigilant; listening for that still small voice; obeying the prompting of the Holy Spirit and the voice of our recreated spirit—the voice of our conscience—to win the battle within.

Through the Process of Avoiding Temptation, we guard against giving up the fruit of the Spirit; watching for strong desires.

Lead us not into the temptation, but deliver us from evil, prepares us for the upsets; giving the Prayer of Imprecation the power to deliver the just out of temptation; being empowered by Jehovah Nissi - the Lord, our Banner

The Prayer of Imprecation

God is an enemy to our enemies and an adversary to our adversaries.

Proverbs 2:10-11
- Wisdom (what): *"When wisdom enters into your heart:* [God has spoken a word to your spirit.]
- Understanding (why): *and knowledge is pleasant to your soul,* [Another logical thought enters your mind.]
- Knowledge (how): *Discretion shall preserve you...,* [You are now wrestling with the flesh.]"

In Exodus 23:22, God told Moses that if the Israelites obey His voice and do all that He speaks, then He would be an enemy unto their enemies and an adversary unto their adversaries. God makes that happen through prayers of Imprecation. These prayers are <u>not</u> directed toward flesh and blood, but flesh (the enemy) only, as we wrestle not against flesh and blood.[23] These prayers lift up the shield of faith to quench all the fiery darts of the wicked:

"O LORD my God, in thee do I put my trust: save me from all them that persecute me, and deliver me: Lest he tear my soul like a lion, rending it in pieces, while there is none to deliver" (Psalms 7:1-2).

"My defense is of God...And God is angry with the wicked every day" (Psalms 7:10-11).

"Evening, and morning, and at noon, will I pray, and cry aloud: and he shall hear my voice. He hath delivered my soul in peace from the battle that was against me: for there were many with me. God shall hear, and afflict them, even he that abideth of old. Selah..." (Psalms 55:17-19).

"Give ear to my prayer, O God; and hide not thyself from my supplication. Attend unto me, and hear me: I mourn in my complaint, and make a noise; <u>Because of the voice of the enemy, because of the oppression of the wicked</u>: for they cast iniquity upon me, and in wrath they hate me" (Psalms 55:1-3).

Being Preserved by Discretion

Proverbs, the book of wisdom, tells us to use discretion[24] when battling the flesh. Solomon says that when God sows a word of wisdom in our hearts, it will often be intercepted by the flesh; offering us a logical alternative to address the same issue but using the natural means. And if it can't *stop* you, it will try to *hinder* you from doing God's will by faith.

To be preserved by discretion, you will need *intel*: being alert and on watch for random thoughts. It is a call to occupy.

Leading with the body:

I was prompted by the Holy Spirit to pick up my brother's prescription. I jumped up in preparation of following the dictates of my heart, but I was stopped by another thought telling me that *I should call first to see if it is in*; adding, *I wouldn't want to make a trip for nothing.* Nevertheless, I followed my spirit, went without calling, and his prescription was ready.

On another occasion, I had to return some Christmas lights that were not working properly. I thought that I would kill two birds with one stone by also picking up some dinner. The problem was, the two destinations were in opposite directions. Then I was reminded by the Holy Spirit that a franchise of the same store was also located next to the restaurant. I thought, *great.*

But as I was preparing to make the trip, the flesh said that I would have to take the lights back to the original store that I bought them from—reasoning that because I didn't have a receipt, the clerk would recognize me and take the item back with no problem. This idea sounded logical, but there was no faith in it. So I chose discretion, and I followed my faith. The clerk at the new store took the item back, without a receipt.

Recently, I went to purchase my favorite color of lipstick. I told the clerk the name of the lipstick; then I found myself reaching into my purse to pay for it. The clerk returned to the counter informing me that she could not find the color. I had noticed that, by faith, my hand had reached for my charge card. Politely, I asked her to allow me to check, and she agreed. I had no trouble locating my color.

According to Romans 12:1-2, we are to present our bodies as a living sacrifice... then renew the mind. By focusing, we present our bodies as a living sacrifice under the influence of the Holy Spirit.

Second guessing:

When Andrew, one of the disciples of Jesus, reported to Him that there was a lad with five loaves of bread and two fish, the *flesh* tried to steal his faith by saying, *"But, what are they among so many?"* [25] Here the flesh was attempting to get him to second-guess himself and focus on the natural. Yet, Jesus fed about five thousand.

The schoolmaster:

I asked my young son to close the venetian blinds. As he proceeded to walk to the window, the *flesh* said to tell him to pull the cord on the right side of the blind. But I held my peace. Without further prompting, his own spirit led him to the correct side and the correct cord. By usurping our authority and wisdom, the flesh is saying, "Don't let them use their faith, tell them what and how to do it."

Searching for broken lines of defense—turning:

When we find ourselves being tempted, using dishonest scales (giving weight to the wrong thing), searching for a speck in our brother's eye (judging another man's servant), being a judge of evil thoughts (watching for infractions of the rules), or being restricted by our emotions, it is the flesh. It is watching for a halting response (broken line of defense)—a means by which it can prevail against us. It is endeavoring to get us to *turn* from faith.

Mind watch:

My son tells the story of taking an exam and feeling really good about his answers. He jumped up to turn in his exam, but he was interrupted by a thought saying: *You had better check your answers, just to make sure.* Unaware that this was his flesh talking (un-renewed mind), he <u>turned</u> and went back to his seat to follow this wisdom (from below) and changed some answers that he was not sure about. When his paper was graded, his score went from an A to a B. He had forgotten a key principle of crucifying the flesh: Swear by your own hurt and change not. This act of *turning* made him double-minded.

The Inner Giant—in his own words:

"And our adversaries said, They shall not know, neither see, till we come in the midst *among them, and slay them, and cause the work to cease"* (Nehemiah 4:11).

"...All my familiars watched for my halting, saying, Peradventure he will be enticed, and we shall prevail against him, and we shall take our revenge on him" (Jeremiah 20:10).

Watch and pray:

To avoid entering into temptation, we are called to watch and pray. We do not want to be found, 'not thinking.' To hinder the work of faith, the enemy may *even* operate as an 'angel of light.' He comes immediately to steal the Word of: knowledge, wisdom, or an instruction sown in our hearts. His goal is disappointment. But watching takes away his element of surprise. The Bible says: *"...in vain is a net spread in the sight of any bird."* (Proverbs 1:17) We also watch to align our prayers to the will of God and His timing. But when we miss it, we just count it all joy!

Playing both ends:

To avoid being disappointed, sometimes you may have to play both ends against the middle, just to stay in faith. I learned this concept from Ecclesiastes 11:6: *"In the morning sow thy seed, and in the evening withhold not thine hand: for thou knowest not whether shall prosper, either this or that, or whether they both shall be alike good."* Earlier in my walk with God and in violation of this principle, it took me weeks to get back on course. After that I was a fast learner.

On one occasion, while preparing to walk by faith, I was prompted to go to a certain car dealership; frustrated with the process, I began to doubt if I had heard from God. So, I started considering another dealership. God prompted me to do both: in the morning sow your seed, in the evening withhold not your hands. So I did, but the first one was God. I got the one with all the bells and whistles. My faith was just being tested.

Thought-counter-thought—look both ways:

As with Samson, the flesh does not know when our *hair* has grown back—when our faith has grown. My son's next flesh attack came about two weeks later. But this time he was watching and praying. He was confident that he would ace the next exam. After completing the main portion of the exam, he was presented with a bonus question. The flesh told him, *You already got them all correct; you don't need to do the bonus question.* My son's counter-thought was, *I need to do the whole test... endure till the end.* He did and it turned out that that the bonus question was needed to help secure his grade of A.

The Holy Spirit told me that this strategy is the same as *looking both ways before crossing.* Before acting on a thought, be armed with a counter-thought. Look both ways. Solomon calls this, *discretion.* Jesus countered each thought, during the temptation, with, *"It is written.*

Jehovah Nissi - the Lord our Banner

Exodus 17:8-15

Through Jehovah Nissi we display the banner of love, and love never fails to deliver the goods. He is there to help us to fight the carnal man, the lusts that war in our members, and the fiery darts of the wicked.

Jehovah Nissi was there:

In Luke 11:6-10, the story is told of a man who asked a friend to lend him three loaves. He told him that the reason was because he had nothing to set before another friend, who in his journey, had come to him. The Bible said that he from <u>within</u> shall answer and say, *"Trouble me not: the door is now shut, and my children are with me in bed; I cannot rise and give thee."* The man, in effect, said: *My flesh said no.* Yet the friend *did* receive the loaves he requested. Through Jehovah Nissi, he refused to give up the fruit of *patience*. He persisted in prayer and troubled his flesh. Our treasure is to persist, as consistency weakens the flesh. By avoiding the temptation to give up the fruit, the loaves were released. With this act, he operated in the Process of Avoiding Temptation.

Jehovah Nissi was there for Daniel:

Daniel placed his relationship with God, above man. When his faith was tested, he was found faithful. The Bible said innocency was found in him, not pride; he did not judge those responsible for his plight. He kept his heart clean. After being thrown into the lion's den, God gave him favor with the king. The king told Daniel that the Lord, whom he served continuously, would deliver him. Daniel allowed Jehovah Nissi to defend him, and God's defense shut the mouths of the lions. Daniel was unharmed because he guarded his heart and held his peace. (Daniel 6)

Jehovah Nissi
Promises Kept in His Name

❖ Because the Lord is your Banner: *"No weapon that is formed against thee shall prosper; and every tongue that shall rise against thee in judgment thou shalt condemn. This is the heritage of the servants of the LORD, and their righteousness is of me, saith the LORD"* (Isaiah 54:17).

❖ Because the Lord is your Banner: *"Thine hand shall find out all thine enemies: thy right hand shall find out those that hate thee"* (Psalms 21:8).

❖ Because the Lord is your Banner: *"Thou hast given a banner to them that fear thee, that it may be displayed because of the truth. Selah. That thy beloved may be delivered; save with thy right hand, and hear me"* (Psalms 60:4-5).

❖ Because the Lord is your Banner: *"He brought me to the banqueting house, and his banner over me was love"* (Song of Solomon 2:4).

❖ Because the Lord is your Banner: *"And having spoiled principalities and powers, he made a shew of them openly, triumphing over them in it"* (Colossians 2:15).

❖ Because the Lord is your Banner: *"...Fear not: for they that be with us are more than they that be with them"* (2 Kings 6:16).

❖ Because the Lord is your Banner: *"Many waters cannot quench love, neither can the floods drown it: if a man would give all the substance of his house for love, it would utterly be contemned"* (Song of Solomon 8:7).

Call to Action:

1. Ask God to show you areas where you have yielded to unbelief and to cleanse you from secret faults.

2. The Armour of God: *"Put on the whole armour of God that ye may be able to stand against the wiles of the devil...* Ephesians 6:12;13-18

3. Ask Him to keep you back from presumptuous sins; let them not have dominion over you; then shall you be upright and innocent from the great transgression.

Pray:
I set my affections on things above, not on things of this earth. (Colossians 3:2)

Confess:
"And having spoiled principalities and powers, he made a show of them openly, triumphing over them in it" (Colossians 2:15).

Chapter 6

1. Galatians 5:17
3. Proverbs 14:12
3. 1 Samuel 18:11-12
4. 1 Samuel 22:2; 2 Samuel 23:8-39
5. Judges 6:15;12
6. Acts 16:27
7. 2 Samuel 3:27-33
8. 1 Samuel 17
9. Proverbs 1:32
10. Genesis 49:3
11. Genesis 49:4
12. Hebrews 4:1-2
13. Genesis 49:22
14. Judges 13-16
15. 1 Corinthians 9:24-27
16. Romans 8:9
17. Galatians 5:18
18. Galatians 5:25
19. Hebrews 11:32
20. Galatians 5:26
21. Nehemiah 4:9
22. Philippians 4:8
23. Ephesians 6:12
24. Proverbs 2:10-11;12-22
25. John 6:8-10

For thine is the kingdom,
and the power, and the glory,
for ever. Amen.

Chapter 7

Deliverance through Joy

*F*or thine is the kingdom, and the power, and the glory, for ever. Amen, evokes the Prayer of Praise and Worship; magnifying God with a spirit of celebration because of what is coming! Through this prayer we call on Jehovah Salome - the Lord our Peace, to guard our harvest. The strategy for this petition is to count it all our joy. Operating the Process of Due Season, we start by not being weary.

Like the children of Israel, some individuals are just not thankful; they can't see the forest for the trees. They say to God, "You parted the Red Sea, but that's not enough." They won't fight the negative voices, and their days are spent in mourning.

Being inspired by the Holy Spirit, I said to one particular individual who was having a great pity party, "I'm sorry that you never got the chance to go to college."

He responded, "I graduated from college."

"Oh," I said, "well I'm sorry you never bought a home."

"What are you talking about?" he answered. "I own my home."

"Oh," I said again, "well I'm sorry that you your children are not doing well."

"My children are fine."

"But wasn't your car stolen?" I asked.

"No," he responded, "where are you getting all of this stuff from?"

Because this man's *focus* was redirected, that conversation effectively turned him from darkness to light.[1]

The Hindrance to the Petition
(Lack of Joy)

We miss it on this level when we fail to count it all joy; [2] instead we focus on vain imaginations. These *lying vanities* place us in the natural—alienated from our spiritual blessings in heavenly places. They seek to cause us to cast away our confidence and its reward.[3] They work vehemently to steal our joy, the strength of our inner man. Without joy, the harvest of the field perishes, *"... even all the trees of the field wither because joy is withered away from the sons of men."* [4]

Either we serve God with joy, or we will serve the enemy with sorrow. Deuteronomy 28:47-48, explains it this way: *"Because thou served not the LORD thy God with joyfulness, and with gladness of heart, for the abundance of all things; Therefore shalt thou serve thine enemies which the LORD shall send against thee, in hunger, and in thirst, and in nakedness, and in want of all things: and he shall put a yoke of iron upon thy neck, until he have destroyed thee."*

The enemy says: buy this vision, thought, idea, or image. When we do, we find ourselves serving our enemies in dry places — for where there is no joy, our enemies reign.

And, once we are taken captive by our enemies, we are *required* to speak out our doubt and unbelief and *bemoan* our sorrows. Psalms 137:3 says: *"...they that carried us away captive required of us a song; they that wasted us required of us mirth."* We are required to share our war stories with others; a type of testimony; however, these stories glorify our enemies: Sing one of those 'somebody did somebody wrong songs.' They want us to get this sorrow into our hearts and rehearse it often. A man of 72, singing his woes, said, "I remember when my baby brother was born, that I was no longer the center of my mother's attention."

Because of lack of joy we serve our enemies.

Lack of Joy—Serving the Enemy

Serving the enemy in hunger:

The Symptom: lack of *self* control
The Cause: not seeking the Lord
The Result: the soul faints for hunger

Because of lack of joy, the hungry soul serves the enemy in murmuring, complaining, and in discontent. Although the prodigal son could have filled his belly with the husks that the swine did eat, he realized that he would still perish with hunger—his soul would not be satisfied. Being idle, it suffered hunger. His soul longed for the fruit of the field and fainted for the courts of the Lord. The prodigal son <u>came to him*self,*</u> repented, and returned home. (Luke 15:11-32)

Serving the enemy in thirst:

The Symptom: a soul given to appetite
The Cause: the lack of good news
The Result: the soul faints for thirst

Because of lack of joy, the thirsty soul is given to appetite. A woman of Samaria, who had been married five times, came to Jacob's well to draw water; there, she met Jesus. He got her attention when He said that whosoever drinks of the water that I shall give him, shall never <u>thirst</u>. Although Jacob's well supplied her with water, it could not give her peace regarding her past; it had no ability to satisfy her soul in drought. Jesus promised that when we believe on Him we shall never thirst. The woman left her water pot and went and <u>shared the good news</u>. (John 4)

Serving the enemy in nakedness:

The Symptom: a fruitless soul; uncovered
The Cause: drunk; walking in the imagination of their hearts
The Result: the soul sighs, groans and mourns

Because of lack of joy, this soul drives drunk. Being uncovered, it is fruitless and therefore unguarded. When Noah drank of the wine of his vineyard, he became drunk and was uncovered within his tent. This action caused Noah to become naked and rendered him fruitless and defenseless. Because his shame was seen, it even became a stumbling block for his younger son, Ham. However, being covered with love, Noah awoke from his wine, rendered judgment, and blessed his older sons. (Genesis 9:21-27)

Serving the enemy in want (lack) of all things:

The Symptom: a soul in distress
The Cause: a famine of hearing the Word of the Lord
The Result: poverty stricken

Because of lack of joy, this soul is in dire straits. When Jesus said unto Simon, *"Launch out into the deep, and let down your nets for a draught."* Simon answered saying, *"Master, we have toiled all the night and taken nothing; nevertheless at thy word I will let down the net."* They then caught a multitude of fishes. Their lack was not for bread, nor for thirst of water, but of hearing a Word from the Lord. They lacked vision: wisdom, instruction, and understanding from the Lord. The Bible said they forsook all, and followed him. (Luke 5; Amos 8:11; Proverbs 23:23)

The Strategy to Escape the Hindrance
(Count it all Joy)

The Bible says when God hears, *"...the voice of joy, and the voice of gladness, the voice of the bridegroom, and the voice of the bride, the voice of them that shall say, Praise the LORD of hosts: for the LORD is good; for his mercy endureth for ever: and of them that shall bring the sacrifice of praise into the house of the LORD. For I will cause to return the captivity of the land, as at the first, saith the LORD"* (Jeremiah 33:11). God wants to return us to the joy of our salvation.

When we have been faithful over a few things, God then endeavors to make us *ruler* over *many things*: the *many* afflictions coming against us and the *many* things that we are careful and troubled about. But the joyfulness test must be passed first. You see, faithfulness makes you ruler over a few things, but joy makes you ruler over *many* things. And, to be joyful, James 1:2 says we will have to learn how to count it all joy.

This is what Jesus must have done during His passion. He had to *prove the promise* that joy would make Him *ruler* (over many things). The crucifixion process starts the countdown:

- First they lied: Jesus said: Joy One!

- The crowd cried: crucify   Jesus said: Joy Two!

- Condemned to die: Jesus said: Joy Three!

- They strung Him high: Jesus said: Joy Four!

- They stretched Him wide: Jesus said: Joy Five!

- His mother cried: Jesus said: Joy Six!

- He hung His head: Jesus said: Joy Seven!

127

- Then He died: Jesus said: Joy Eight!

- They pierced His side: Jesus yelled: Joy Nine!

- He rose again: Jesus said: Joy Ten...

I endured to the end!

No matter what level Jesus was attacked on, He was sustained by joy:

Rejected by the crowd—He was sustained by joy.

Emotionally torn by His mother's tears—He was sustained by joy.
Forsaken by His friends—He was sustained by joy.

Stricken, smitten of God, and afflicted—He was sustained by joy.

In the Book of Revelation, Jesus, said: *"I am He that liveth, and was dead, and <u>behold,</u> I am alive forever more, Amen; and I have the keys to hell and death."* 5 Through the death, burial and resurrection of the cross, Jesus broke the power of the enemy. Because of joy, is He not King of kings, Lord of lords, and indeed, Ruler over many things? Jesus did it for the joy that was set before Him. Joy enabled Jesus to endure the cross by despising the shame—He saw the shame as little or nothing at all. We can too.

Prayer Stance

Prayer Stance is the <u>posture</u> we should take *following prayer* to insure our harvest. But first, we must acknowledge that a change has taken place. In 1 Samuel 1, Hannah was a woman of a sorrowful spirit; she was in bitterness of soul. She wanted a child but was barren. The Bible said that her adversary provoked her bitterly. Finally, she went to the temple, prayed, and asked God for a child; vowing to lend him to the Lord all the days of his life.

After Hannah poured out her soul before the Lord, nothing changed in the natural. Nevertheless, the Bible says, her 'countenance was no more sad.' [6] Her prayer had caused her inner man to stand.

Prayer stance one: We are no more sad

Hannah exemplifies the number one prayer stance. We are to verbally acknowledge that our countenance is no more sad. Our spirt is affected when we perform the duty of prayer.

When prayers are made according to the will of God, He hears us, and if we *know* that He hears us, we know we have the petition we have desired of Him. [7]

Prayer stance two: Joy of faith

According to 1 Peter, joy allows us to see the end of our faith; even the salvation of our souls. [8] It allows us to keep a spirit of celebration because of what's coming.

In 2 Kings 3, the story is told of King Jehoram who was having trouble with another king (King Moab). So, he asked King Jehoshaphat to go with him to war against Moab. The king of Edom went along also.

Now, to fully understand this story you will have to understand the role each king is playing. Remember, the Old Testament is written in types and shadows. Therefore, the good king

(Jehoshaphat) represents the *spirit of man*; King Jehoram represents the *soul of man*; the king of Edom represents the *body of man*. Also, the king of Moab represents the *flesh,* and Elisha represents himself (*the man of God*).

The Bible says that as they travelled, they ran out of water for their men and cattle. Jehoshaphat suggested that they ask the prophet for help. So, Elisha came, analyzed the situation, and he realized that they had faith, but joy was missing. They had not entered into the joy of the Lord; therefore, they had no strength.[9] Elisha knew something about faith that the kings didn't know: First, he knew that faith needs partners; it can't 'stand' being alone. Second, he knew that faith is picky; it is particular about who it will work with. Through grace, faith is looking for one of three partners: love, patience, or joy.

When you give faith a partner, faith will: subdue kingdoms, work righteousness, obtain promises, stop the mouths of lions, quench the violence of fire, enable you to escape the edge of the sword, ensure that out of weakness you will be made strong, and ensure that you will be victorious in fight. Also, faith will turn to flight the armies of the aliens, and those who are dead in trespasses and sin, will faith raise to life again. And if you don't get what you want, faith will give you a better resurrection. [10] The women who went to anoint the body of Jesus did not get to do what they wanted to do, but they were able to witness a risen Savior; [11] they received a better resurrection.

Elisha realized that to win this type of battle, the kings needed what Paul called, *'joy of faith.'* [12] Joy may be described as a calm delight; a delight of the mind; [13] a glorious and triumphant state...all to the expectation of good. Joy is an antidote, and it is the only remedy that can give us immediate release from the negativity of life.

Joy is a fruit of the Spirit that emanates from the nature of God. It is a part of our born again spirit; independent of circumstances and self-sustaining. It is an offensive weapon; the ball is in your court. When joy is present, it places us in the presence of

God and annihilates the enemy. Joy will not only cause your mouth to be enlarged over your enemy, joy is required to draw water out of the well of salvation.14 Finally, when you take joyfully the spoiling of your goods, stolen things will be returned to you.15

But joy must be cultivated, sowed for, and reaped. So we need to leap for joy, rejoice for joy, shout for joy, and sing for joy. Unlike rejoicing, which focuses on the past, and unlike happiness, which is based on emotions that are subject to change, joy's focus is on the future of things to come—the expectation of good. And the Bible says our expectations shall not be cut off. 16 Joy will cause us to rejoice at the plumb line and rejoice at the blade.

The Bible also says that joy is the weapon that allows us to see the end of our faith, even the salvation of our souls. So, Elisha, perfecting what was lacking in the kings' faith, called for a musician. As the musician played, joy filled the air and the people began praising God. All they could think about was the expectation of good and the abundance of things to come. The more they thought about it, they began leaping for joy, rejoicing for joy, shouting for joy, and singing for joy. The Father, being pleased with their joy of faith, gave them double for their trouble. He promised not only water but victory as well! Their prayer brought them to God, and their joy brought God to them!

The next morning the sun arose. As it was shining over the water, it gave it a reddish look. It was just a natural phenomenon, but when the natural is all that you see, the natural view is all that you will ever have. So, walking by sight, the Moabites (flesh) looked at the water and assumed it was blood. They thought the kings had killed themselves. So, they rushed in to what they thought was the spoil, but ran up against the promise that cannot be defeated. And the children of Israel, filled with the joy of faith, partook of the promise and rushed in and defeated them, not just on the battlefield; all the way even into their own country. In other words, after they defeated them, they occupied the enemy's land. The only weapon they had was the joy of faith.

In the 15th verse of Luke, chapter 3, the people were in expectation. In verse 21, Jesus came (to be baptized). He prayed and the heavens were opened. The joy of faith brings the expectation of good—a powerful prayer stance.

Prayer stance three: Involves the element of <u>time</u>

God has already blessed us with all spiritual blessings in heavenly places.[17] The book of Hebrews says: *"The works were finished before the foundation of the world."* [18] This stance declares that we must enter into the finished work of Christ. 1Peter 2:24, addressing the healing promise, says: *"By whose stripes you <u>were</u> healed."*

I had the opportunity to share this prayer stance with a young lady who had an allergic reaction to meds. She had received her healing by faith, but she was concerned about how to deal with the symptoms, if they were still visible by the end of the week. I shared with her that God was not in time. He is in the now; faith is now. Her prayer stance has to be: *I have already received my healing.* She took that stance and the symptoms were gone the next day.

Prayer stance four: Taking captive every thought

Taking captive every thought begins with a <u>watch</u> against the wiles of the tempter.

- Watch for a deceitful tongue...*there are giants in the land*
- Watch for a lying tongue...*God does not love you*
- Watch for a false tongue... *everyone is doing it*
- Watch for the froward tongue...*don't take that*
- Watch for the flattery of the tongue...*yours was the best*
- Watch for a naughty tongue...*no one will know*
- Watch for a backbiting tongue...*he has issues*
- Watch for a perverse tongue...*curse him out*
- Watch for the strife of tongue ...*she's accusing you again!*

I noticed that you were not fighting your thoughts:

The other day while listening to a Bible teacher, I noticed myself becoming alarmed, as well as sad. He was discussing things that were fearful in terms of staying in touch with God. The teacher stated that he was not trying to cause fear, but he did. As I listened I became more and more uneasy; I had no more joy. Finally, the Holy Spirit asked me, "Why are you sad?" I explained to him what the man of God was saying: mostly about facing future attacks and missing God.

The Holy Spirit said, "But I am in the future." My joy returned. Later I asked the Holy Spirit how He knew that I was sad. He said it was because He noticed that I was not fighting my thoughts anymore—I had not taken them captive. I quickly returned to my labor in the Word.

Years ago, the Holy Spirit impressed upon me that He was not concerned about *what* the thoughts were saying to me, only about my response to the thoughts.

Taking captive every thought has become a life-line for me. Here is a sample of what this process looks like:

The thought says...	Your response...
God does not love you.	I am the apple of God's eye.
God can't forgive you for that.	I am forgiven by the blood.
God can't use you.	The last shall be first.
But you smoke and drink.	I am healed as I go.
No one will hire you.	I have favor with God and man.
You are sick.	By His stripes I am healed.
You need help.	I am more than a conqueror.

Prayer stance five: Laboring to enter into His rest

God's Alert

Hebrews 4:9-11
- Wisdom (what): *"There remaineth therefore a rest to the people of God.*
- Understanding (why): *For he that is entered into his rest, he also has ceased from his own works, as God did from his.*
- Knowledge (how): *Let us labour therefore to enter into that rest, lest any man fall after the same example of unbelief."*

According to Hebrews, we must *labour* to enter into His rest by holding fast to our profession of faith; keeping the sword by our side. For Abraham, this involved *driving away* the fowls of the air to protect the covenant sacrifice: *"When the fowls came down upon the carcases, Abram drove them away."*[19] John 1:5 says: the Light shines in the darkness and the darkness comprehended it not. Our labor involves shining His light into the restless areas of our souls.

134

Labor number one:

Be patient. The fruit of patience is the sceptre of righteousness that must be employed till due season. Patience is defined as: *That quality or virtue that does not surrender to circumstances or succumb under trials.* The Bible says that the husbandman waits for the precious fruit of the earth. [20] We are not trying to get the promise, we are just guarding it. It is good for a man to both hope and quietly wait for the salvation of the Lord.

Labor number two:

Know your enemy. The flesh weakens with persistence. God told Joshua to meditate day and night on the Word. God would then make his way prosperous and he would have good success.[21]

Labor number three:

Never give up. The Bible says that Joshua drew not back his hand, wherewith he stretched out his spear, until he had utterly destroyed all the inhabitants of Ai. [22]

Labor number four:

Study to show *self* who you are. Prove to the flesh the good, acceptable, and perfect will of God. [23] The Bible calls this faith. The New English Translation says faith is the proving of things not seen. We are to take the Word of Faith and war a mighty warfare. [24] That means we are to pull down strongholds. These may be philosophies, thoughts, or traditions of man that come against the wisdom of God. Then we are to cast down wicked imaginations and bring into captivity every thought to the obedience of Christ—in line with our anointing. This type of mental sanctification is done just to *prove* to ourselves who we are.

We are also to prove, to the flesh, the promises that have been given us. 2 Peter 1:4 says, God has given us exceeding great and precious promises to enable us to be a partaker of His divine nature, so that we may escape the corruption that is in this world, through lust. We must prove we possess that which has been given to us.

Labor number five:

Command your morning. [25] This involves cursing dreams and visions, nets, cords, gins, and snares—the devices and wiles of the enemy, that exalt themselves against the knowledge of God. It also involves pleading the blood, speaking to the mountain, binding and loosing, and interceding for self and others in the spirit. It even calls those things that be not as though they were, as well as casting your care—even legitimate cares, and communicating your faith. [26] Your goal is for the restoration of your peace.

Labor number six:

Guard your heart. Analyze thoughts for virtue.
- Wisdom (what): *"Keep thy heart with all diligence;*
- Understanding (why): *for out of it are the issues of life.*
- Knowledge (how): *Put away from thee a froward mouth, and perverse lips put far from you..."* (Proverbs 4:23-27).

The issues of life flow out from us. When our thoughts are not filled with virtue, the law of the spirit of life in Christ Jesus that has made us free from the law of sin and death, cannot flow; the fruit of the spirit cannot flow. Virtue is released by focusing on thoughts that give us a good report. According to scripture, if your thoughts do not give you a good report, you can't think on them, since there is no virtue in them—no power to produce the good.[27] Moreover, negative words will produce after themselves and bring self-fulling prophesies.

Labor number seven:

Offer the sacrifice of thanksgiving. Jonah's sacrifice of thanksgiving caused the Lord to speak to the fish, and it vomited Jonah upon dry land.[28] The abundance of grace also abounds with thanksgiving. [29]

Labor number eight:

Maintain a spirit of celebration. After being edified by her cousin, Elizabeth, Mary (the mother of Jesus), in anticipation of the promised Seed, does it right. She turned her attention from not being qualified (I know not a man) and took her stance with a spirit of celebration:

(Luke 1:45-47)
- Wisdom (what): *"And blessed is she that believed*
- Understanding (why): *for there shall be a performance of those things told her from the Lord.*
- Knowledge (how): *And Mary said, My Soul does magnify the Lord, And my spirit hath rejoiced in God my Savior."*

Mary's spirit and soul were in alignment which allowed the issues of life to flow—which brought about a manifestation.

Labor number nine:

Beware of the comeback. Plead the Blood. After the children of Israel were set free, the enemy pursued after them saying, *"Why have we done this, that we have let Israel go from serving us"* (Exodus14:5).

The enemy also said, *"I will pursue, I will overtake, I will divide the spoil; my lust shall be satisfied upon them; I will draw my sword, my hand shall destroy them"* (Exodus 15:9). Holding your peace and pleading the blood will address the enemy's return attack.

The Process of Due Season
Seedtime and Harvest

(Guarding Your Harvest)

This process focuses on *not being weary in the race.*

Galatians 6:9
- Wisdom (what): *"Be not deceived; God is not mocked: for whatsoever a man soweth, that shall he also reap*
- Understanding (why): *For he that soweth to his flesh shall of the flesh reap corruption; but he that soweth to the Spirit shall of the Spirit reap life everlasting.*
- Knowledge (how): *And let us not be weary in well doing: for in due season we shall reap, if we faint not."*

A young woman was struggling to quit smoking; to make matters worse, she was a born again, tongue-speaking Christian—highly spiritual. Smoking brought her a great deal of shame. I shared with her the process of due season—informing her of what God told one pastor: that if a person knew that there was a due season (following prayer), they would never worry. She received this revelation and waited for due season. Approximately five years later she received the grace to stop smoking.

To everything there is a season, and to every purpose there is a time. 30 It has been said that we do not lose because the enemy beat us; we lose because we give up. When the incorruptible seed of the Word of God is sown, it never returns void. It always produces fruit; it always accomplishes its goal; it always prospers. According to 1 Kings 8:56, there has not failed one word of all God's good promises; all have come to pass. In Leviticus 26, God promises to give us rain in due season. When our eyes wait upon Him, He gives us meat in due season. 31 And God's Words of promise are fulfilled in their season.

The culprit, however, is weariness—an attempt to hurry the soul. Yet, it is the soul that *needs* the processing time: first the blade, then the corn; after that, the full corn in the year. [32] Our treasure is to endure to the end. How do we answer weariness? Due season.

For Thine is the Kingdom, and the Power, and the Glory, For Ever. Amen

Key elements of this petition:

The Hindrance to this petition lies in becoming weary in well doing. When the heart is troubled, by emotions or vain imaginations, our *house becomes divided and we are found faulty. We have cast off that which is good, an enemy shall pursue us.* (Hosea 8:3; 10:2)

The Strategy calls for us to count it all joy. Joy guards our harvest, bringing God on the scene, which transfers the battle. Joy is also required to draw water out of the well of salvation, giving us: deliverance, protection, healing, and preservation.

Through the Process of Due Season, we shall reap, if we faint not. In Joel 2:25, God promised to restore to us the years that the locust hath eaten. And, in Jeremiah 33:9-14, the Lord promises to give prosperity and peace, as He restores fortunes. God says: *"...and they shall fear and tremble for all the goodness and for all the prosperity that I procure unto it...Behold, the days come, saith the LORD, that I will perform that good thing which I have promised unto the house of Israel and to the house of Judah."*

For thine is the kingdom, and the power, and the glory, for ever. Amen, speaks of the delight of God performing His marital duties on our behalf; giving the Prayer of Praise and Worship the power to release God's strength into the battle to bring in our harvest; being empowered by Jehovah Salome - the Lord our Peace.

Prayer of Praise and Worship

These prayers execute judgment on the enemy and bring in the harvest:

Psalms 149:6-9

- Wisdom (what): *"Let the high praises of God be in their mouth and a two-edged sword in their hand;*
- Understanding (why): *to execute vengeance upon the heathen, and punishments upon the people; To bind their kings with chains, and their nobles with fetters of iron; To execute upon them the judgment written: this honour have all his saints.*
- Knowledge (how): *Praise ye the LORD."*

"All thy works shall praise thee, O LORD; and thy saints shall bless thee. They shall speak of the glory of thy kingdom and talk of thy power" (Psalms 145:10-11).

"Wherefore David blessed the LORD before all the congregation: and David said, Blessed be thou, LORD God of Israel our father, for ever and ever. Thine, O LORD, is the greatness, and the power, and the glory, and the victory, and the majesty: for all that is in the heaven and in the earth is thine; thine is the kingdom, O LORD, and thou art exalted as head above all. Both riches and honour come of thee, and thou reignest over all; and in thine hand is power and might; and in thine hand it is to make great, and to give strength unto all. Now therefore, our God, we thank thee, and praise thy glorious name" (1 Chronicles 29:10-13—<u>A corollary to the Lord's Prayer</u>).

Jehovah Salome - the Lord our Peace

Judges 6:24

Jehovah Salome brings us into a state of peace; declaring nothing missing, nothing broken. He is there to guide our feet into the way of peace. He shall also give us an answer of peace; silencing the enemy of our souls.

Jehovah Salome was there for Gideon:

In Judges 6, Gideon considered himself to be the least in his father's house. But God called him a mighty man of valor. The Lord also informed him that he was being called to save Israel from the Midianites. How? The Lord answered, *"Surely I will be with you."* Gideon discovered that when Jehovah Salome - the Lord our Peace, is there, you can defeat the enemy as one man. 33 When Gideon and his men operated from a posture of peace, the Bible said the enemy ran, cried, and fled as every man stood in his place of authority. With their feet were shod with the preparation of the gospel of peace, the enemy was subdued; and they lifted up their heads no more. With this act, Gideon operated in the Process of Seedtime and Harvest.

Jehovah Salome was there for the disciples:

In Mark 4:35-39, Jesus went into a ship with His disciples and told them, *"Let us pass over to the other side. And there arose a great storm of wind.* [The storm came as soon as the Word was spoken; as the enemy came to steal the Word that had been sown in their hearts.] *Jesus was asleep* [for the teacher is quiet during the test] they awake Him and say unto Him, Master, carest thou not that we perish? *He arose, and rebuked, the wind and said to the sea, Peace be still. And the wind ceased, and there was a great calm."* Even when we are faint, Jehovah Salome is there to quiet the storm.

Jehovah Salome
Promises Kept in His Name

❖ Because the Lord is your Peace: *"Thou wilt keep him in perfect peace, whose mind is stayed on thee: because he trusteth in thee"* (Isaiah 26:3).

❖ Because the Lord is your Peace: *"The LORD shall fight for you, and ye shall hold your peace"* (Exodus 14:14).

❖ Because the Lord is your Peace: *"Mark the perfect man, and behold the upright: for the end of that man is peace"* (Psalms 37:37).

❖ Because the Lord is your Peace: *"Great peace have they which love thy law: and nothing shall offend them"* (Psalms 119:165).

❖ Because the Lord is your Peace: *"He maketh peace in thy borders, and filleth thee with the finest of the wheat"* (Psalms 147:14).

❖ Because the Lord is your Peace: *"When a man's ways please the LORD, he maketh even his enemies to be at peace with him"* (Proverbs 16:7).

❖ Because the Lord is your Peace: *"And let the peace of God rule in your hearts, to the which also ye are called in one body; and be ye thankful"* (Colossians 3:15).

Call to Action:

1. Ask God to help you enter into His rest, as the works were finished from the foundation of the world. Ask Him to help you labour to enter into that rest, lest you fall after the same example of unbelief.

2. *"Awake, awake; put on thy strength, O Zion; put on thy beautiful garments, O Jerusalem, the holy city: for henceforth there shall no more come into thee the uncircumcised and the unclean"* (Isaiah 52:1).

3. Do not be weary in well doing; you shall reap if you faint not.

Pray:
Pray that you endure to the end; see the end of your faith; even the salvation of your soul. Thank God for due season.

Confess:
Finally, offer the sacrifice of thanksgiving. Say the following: *"...my heart rejoiceth in the LORD, mine horn is exalted in the LORD: my mouth is enlarged over mine enemies; because I rejoice in thy salvation. There is none holy as the LORD: for there is none beside thee: neither is there any rock like our God,"* (1 Samuel 2:1-2).

Chapter 7

1. Acts 26:18
2. James 1:2
3. Hebrews 10:35
4. Joel 1:12
5. Revelation 1:18
6. 1 Samuel 1:18
7. 1 John 5:14-15
8. 1 Peter 1:8-9
9. Nehemiah 8:10
10. Hebrews 11:33-35
11. Matthews 28:1-7
12. Philippians 1:25
13. Webster's 1828 Dictionary
14. Isaiah 12:3
15. Hebrews 10:34
16. Proverbs 23:18
17. Ephesians 1:3
18. Hebrews 4:3
19. Genesis 15:11
20. James 5:7
21. Joshua 1:8
22. Joshua 8:26
23. Romans 12:2
24. 1 Timothy 1:18
25. Job 38:12
26. Philemon 1:6
27. Philippians 4:8
28. Jonah 2:7-10
29. 2 Corinthians 4:15
30. Ecclesiastes 3:1
31. Psalms 145:15
32. Mark 4:28
33. Judges 6:16

Appendix

Prayer Alert

- Wisdom (what): *"Be not therefore like unto them.*
- Understanding (why): *For Your Father knows what things you have need of before you ask Him.*
- Knowledge (how): *After this manner, pray ye...*

Our Father which art in heaven, Hallowed be thy name.
Thy kingdom come.
Thy will be done in earth, as it is in heaven.
Give us this day our daily bread.
And forgive us our debts, as we forgive our debtors.
And lead us not into temptation, but deliver us from evil:
For thine is the kingdom, and the power, and the glory,
for ever. Amen." (Matthew 6:8-13).

Rx: The Lord's Prayer should be a part of your daily prayer regimen. It should be prayed at the beginning of your day; also as needed, throughout the day.

Begin by putting on the armour of God (Ephesians 6:11-18); followed by the Lord's Prayer, its Corollary and Confessions of Faith. Pray Psalms 91 for divine protection. Pray Ephesians 1:16-19; 3:14-20, for the eyes of your understanding to be enlightened. Pray Psalms 23 to feed the soul and end with Psalms 5:12, for divine favor. Be blessed!

Praying: The Lord's Prayer
Its Corollary and Confessions of Faith

Our Father which art in heaven, Hallowed be thy name: *Thine, O LORD, is the greatness, and the power, and the glory, and the victory, and the majesty: for all that is in the heaven and in the earth is thine;*

Thy kingdom come: *Thine is the kingdom, O LORD, and thou art exalted as head above all...I am the head, not the tail.*

Thy will be done in earth, as it is in heaven: *Both riches and honour come of thee, and thou reignest over all;*

Give us this day our daily bread: *And in thine hand is power and might...Death and life are in the power of the tongue.*

And forgive us our debts, as we forgive our debtors: *And in thine hand it is to make great...thy gentleness (kindness) has made me great.*

And lead us not into temptation, but deliver us from evil: *and to give strength unto all...I put on my strength, my beautiful garment of praise. I wait upon You, You renew my strength.*

For thine is the kingdom, and the power, and the glory, for ever. Amen: *Now therefore, our God, we thank thee, and praise thy glorious name: You are Jehovah Shammah; You are always there for me. Jehovah Tsidkenu, my Righteousness. Jehovah Jireh, my Provider. Jehovah Rohi, my Shepherd. Jehovah Nissi, Your Banner over me is love. Jehovah Rapha, my Healer. And You are Jehovah Salome, my Peace that surpasses all understanding. Father, in Jesus Name, I cast the whole of my care on You; I commit my way unto You. I yield my will to do Your will; I pray for those You have placed on my heart. I touch and agree for Your blessings to manifest. Amen.*

The Lord's Prayer—Revisited
Chapter Guide

The following are elements included in chapters 1-7

Chapter 1
Petition: *Our Father which art in heaven, Hallowed be thy name.*
Redemptive Name: Jehovah Shammah - the Lord is There
Type of Prayer: Prayer of Agreement
The Hindrance: King is a Child
The Strategy to Escape the Hindrance: Sonship
The Process: Discernment Agreement-Calling and Naming

Chapter 2
Petition: *Thy kingdom come.*
Redemptive Name: Jehovah Rohi - the Lord our Shepherd
Type of Prayer: Prayer of Commitment
The Hindrance: The Hungry Soul
The Strategy to Escape the Hindrance: Feeding the Hungry Soul
The Process: Overcoming-Buying and Selling

Chapter 3
Petition: *Thy will be done in earth, as it is in heaven.*
Redemptive Name: Jehovah Tsidkenu - the Lord our Righteousness
Type of Prayer: Prayer of Consecration
The Hindrance: Doubtful Mind
The Strategy to Escape the Hindrance: The Willing Mind
The Process: Occupying-Hearing and Keeping

Chapter 4
Petition: *Give us this day, our daily bread.*
Redemptive Name: Jehovah Jireh - the Lord our Provider
Type of Prayer: Prayer of Petition; Prayer of Faith
The Hindrance: Unruly Tongue
The Strategy to Escape the Hindrance: Taming the Tongue
The Process: Effectual Prayer-Believing and Receiving

Chapter 5
Petition: *Forgive us our debts, as we forgive our debtors.*
Redemptive Name: Jehovah Rapha - the Lord our Healer
Type of Prayer: Prayer of Confession
The Hindrance: Unclean Heart
The Strategy to Escape the Hindrance: The Love Walk
The Process: Dominion-Binding and Loosing

Chapter 6
Petition: *Lead us not into temptation, but deliver us from evil:*
Redemptive Name: Jehovah Nissi - the Lord our Banner
Type of Prayer: Prayer of Imprecation
The Hindrance: Flesh: Inner Giant
The Strategy to Escape the Hindrance: Fruit of the Spirit
The Process: Avoiding Temptation-Watching and Praying

Chapter 7
Petition: *For thine is the kingdom, and the power, and the glory, for ever. Amen.*
Redemptive Name: Jehovah Salome - the Lord our Peace
Type of Prayer: Prayer of Praise and Worship;
The Hindrance: Lack of Joy
The Strategy to Escape the Hindrance: Count it all Joy
The Process: Due Season-Seedtime and Harvest

The Lord's Prayer-Revisited
7 Ways to Deliverance

Checklist

Put a check mark next to your confession of faith...

#1	I pray as a son/daughter		I am guarding my identity. I am discerning good and bad.	
#2	I minister to my soul		I am guarding my soul. My heart is inditing a good matter.	
#3	I have a willing mind		I am guarding my will. There is a performance.	
#4	I am believing I received		I am guarding the promise. I have bridled my tongue.	
#5	I have a clean heart		I am guarding my peace. I owe no man nothing but love.	
#6	I am avoiding temptation		I am guarding my fruit. I am watchful.	
#7	I am counting it all joy		I am guarding the harvest. I am not fainting.	

Other books by Carolyn Chambers

DISCOVERING YOUR ANOINTING NUMBERS

By Carolyn Chambers

In her life-changing new book, Carolyn Chambers helps readers discover their anointing numbers and empower them to fight life's great battle-themselves. Simply put—everyone is at war with *self*. But walking anointed is something everyone can achieve. In, "Discovering Your Anointing Numbers: Allow me to introduce you to Yourself," Carolyn Chambers examines the influence that birth demographics have on human behavior. This is a compelling read for all.

THE ANOINTED LIFE-*Crucifying the Flesh*

By Carolyn Chambers

Thoughts received from the flesh alienate us from the grace of God; while those from the spirit bring righteousness, peace, and joy. The flesh cunningly attacks the will, the mind, and the emotions; keeping us in a place of immaturity and alienated from our inheritance through fear, doubt, and unbelief. But thoughts received from the spirit position us to live the anointed life—a life lived under the influence of the Holy Spirit.

Also from Anointed Life Publishing

SKI

By Al Sutton

The war did not end for Ralph. It resumes on even the slightest provocation: A tree line on a freeway instantly becomes a place where enemy fire erupts from, and rain brings back vivid memories of the horrors of war in the jungles of Vietnam. The pain is so intense that Ralph decides to do something that the very people he fought for will never forget. But despite the odds, Ralph discovers a more powerful weapon that will defeat all of his enemies and change his life forever.

PREPARING FOR PRIVATE AND PAROCHIAL SCHOOLS

By Winnie Eke, PhD.

This handbook is designed to help parents through the process of preparing themselves and their children for the challenges that lie ahead. It may not answer all the questions but it will highlight most of the common ones and those that I deem essential. It was inspired as a result of what I, as a parent, went through in the transition to an alternate educational experience with my own children.

We invite you to visit our website at:

Anointed Life Publishing

www.anointinglifepublishing.com

To get information regarding having the author speak at your group, organization, or church, please e-mail us at carolyn.allow@yahoo.com